BRITAIN IS NOW VE

There has never been a vegetarian guide like this one. It features **hundreds** of vegetarian restaurants, cafés, hotels and guest houses all over Britain with:

> opening times
> complete addresses
> phone numbers
> prices
> detailed descriptions
> what's on the menu for vegans
> directions to out of the way places

Whether you're hankering for a day trip or touring the country, a student seeking a bargain buffet or a millionaire looking for luxury, now you can be sure of finding fabulous food at vegetarian eateries and sleeperies.

Co-author **Alex Bourke** worked for a major guidebook publisher from 1985 to 1989 and wrote *The Vegan Guide to Paris* and bestsellling *Vegetarian London*. **Alan Todd** is a publishing consultant for green charities such as Forum for the Future and The International Hotels Environment Initiative. They have also published *Vegetarian France*.

"From Penzance to Peebles, everywhere you need to know for a perfect night out, weekend or holiday." Tina Fox, The Vegetarian Society.

2

Vegetarian Britain
by Alex Bourke and AlanTodd
foreword by Paul & Linda McCartney
published by Vegetarian Guides Ltd, 197 Greyhound Road,
London W14 9SD

ISBN 1-902259 01 7. First published March 1998.

Cover designed by Mark Halunga, 0171-794 1149

Also published simultaneously:
Vegetarian France, £6.99, ISBN 1-902259 00 9

In preparation: Vegetarian Belgium and Holland

Individual copies available from the publishers. See order
form at the end of this guide.

The small print:
Whilst every effort has been made to ensure the accuracy of information contained in this
book, the authors accept no liability for any errors. Acceptance of advertisements does
not imply endorsement of either the advertisers or their products or services. If you would
like to advertise in the next edition, please write to Vegetarian Guides Ltd.

Printed and bound in Great Britain by
Cox & Wyman Ltd, Reading, Berkshire

VEGETARIAN
BRITAIN

over 500 places to eat and sleep

by Alex Bourke and Alan Todd

foreword by Paul & Linda McCartney

published by Vegetarian Guides, London

CONTENTS

Foreword by **Paul & Linda McCartney**

8 North East
Cleveland, Durham, Humberside,
Northumberland, Tyne and Wear, Yorkshire

9 Cumbria (The Lake District)

10 Scotland

11 Wales

Introduction

by

Paul & Linda McCartney

This guide to *Vegetarian Britain* is one of the brightest ideas we've come across in a long time. It's a little cracker of a book which tells you where to find really good vegetarian food - from a snack to a slap up gourmet meal - and it comes with best wishes from both of us.

Paul McCartney

Linda McCartney

BIG Thanks from Alex & Alan to:

Alex at MPL, Geoff Baker, Mike Bourke, Steve Connor, Tina Fox, Katie Fedor, Paul Gaynor, Dr Michael Grill, Karin Gunnarsson, Mark Halunga, Shelagh Jones, Brigitte Kehrwisch, London Vegans, John Milroy, Huong Nguyen, Ian Kirby, Saara Lusher, Paul and Linda McCartney, Paul Mielek, Chris Olivant, Clare Palmer, Rita, Doug Robertson, Ronny, Dr Kasia Siudem, Patrick Smith, Tony Weston, Avery Wham and all our friends and supporters.

We wrote to every place listed in this book and a few more. Unlike some guides we charge ZILCH for listings and are thus totally impartial and comprehensive. Those who ignored our generous offers of free publicity we harassed mercilessly till they finally surrendered their menus. And we asked local veggie gastronauts what they reckoned too. Anywhere with the scantest of listings proved impossible to get a reply from. But you're welcome to it next time around.... purleeeze return our questionnaire or your menu!

Is established 'to promote and carry on the business of producing vegan foods'

PLAMIL non-dairy alternatives to milk are formulated for vegan nutritional requirements, with the correct balance of vegan calcium combined with vitamin D2 to enable the body to absorb the calcium, plus the essential vitamins B12 and B2.

Two varieties: WHITE-SUN (Sunflower/Peas)
1. Apple sweetned 1 litre - Tetrapak
2. No added sugar 1 litre - Tetrapak

Four varieties: (soya)
1. No added sugar 1 litre - Tetrapak
2. Concentrated no added sugar 500ml - Tetrapak
3. Apple sweetened 1 litre - Tetrapak
4. Raw sugar 475ml - easy-open can

RANGE in health stores includes:

Egg-free mayonnaise
Veeze (alternative to cheese spread)
Rice puddings with sultanas
Chocolate bars with soya
Organic chocolates & drops
Carob bars with soya & drops
Carob spreads

NO GENETICALLY ENGINEERED INGREDIENTS
- -
Informative literature - sae to Plamil Foods, Folkestone CT19 6PQ

Name . . . . (BLOCK CAPITALS)

Address . . . .

SOUTH WEST
Avon

Demuths
2 North Parade Passage
Off Abbey Green
Bath
Avon BA1 1NX
Tel: 01225-446 059 Fax: 01225-314 308
Open: Every day 10.00-22.00 (Sat from 09.00)
Vegetarian dishes from all around the world, half of them
vegan and clearly marked, including the desserts. 12 entrées
£2.75-4.95 such as soup, hummus, guacamole, roasted
squash and pumpkin, aubergine red pesto foccacia, nachos,
bruschetta. 3 main course salads £5.25-5.75 like spinach with
avocado and pinenut. 6 main courses £7.75 might be
Koulibiaca Russian vegetable layered pie with wild rice and
pinenuts in puff pastry served with fines herbs sauce and local
vegetables; Indonesian Pecel platter of pickle, spical peanut
sambal, potato with spring onions and chillies in coconut and
lime served with a salad; smoky polenta gratin with salsa rosa.
Vegans, who usually get a lousy deal in the dessert department in 80% of vegetarian restaurants, will think they've land-
ed in heaven. 7 major desserts £3-4 plus loads of lighter ones
include vegan chocolate fudge cake,vegan apple crumble,
vegan sticky treacle pudding with a toffee sauce, luscious
lemon sponge, banoffi pie. They also do vegan chocolate,
strawberry or vanilla soya ice cream and several sorbets, and
even soya milkshakes. House wine £8.50 a bottle or £1.95 a
glass, teas £1.20, coffee £1.05 soya milkshakes. 10% discount to members of the Vegan Society.

Puppet Theater Café

River-side Walk
17 Argyle Street
Bath
Avon BA2 4BQ
Tel: 01225-480 532 Fax:
Open: Mon-Fri 8.30-18.00, Sat-Sun 8-18.00.
Vegetarian with traditional café food. 1 veggie and 1 vegan salad £1.95-3.50. 6 vegan and 10 vegetarian main courses £2.25-3.95 such as pizza, garlic bread with salad and hummus, home made soup with granary bread, ploughman's. 1 vegan and 8 veggie desserts 80p-£2.50 like chocolate fudge cake, hot pecan pie. Wine £10 bottle, £2.25 glass. Tea 80p, coffee 95p. No soya milk. Highchairs, children's portions.

Scoffs Wholefood Café & Bakery

20 Kingsmede Square
Bath
Avon BA1 2AE
Tel: 01225-462 483 Fax:
Open: Mon-Sat 08.00-20.00. Closed Sun.
Wholefood vegetarian café and take-away. 6 vegan and 1 veggie salad 75p-£2.95 like potato, pasta, rice, taboule, spinach and pinto bean. 2 vegan and 6 veggie mains £1.60-2.90 such as spinach turnovers, Homity pies, soup, lasagne, mushroom Bordelaise. All food can be eaten in, with leaf garnish or take-away. Selection of 12 cakes £1. Lots of teas, coffee, cappuchino, hot choc 90p. Soya milk available. 2 highchairs. Wheelchair access. Non-smoking.

Bristol

Arches Hotel

132 Cotham Brow
Cotham
Bristol
Avon BS6 6AE
Tel: 0117-924 7398 Fax: 0117-924 7398
Open all year except Xmas and New Year.
Veg/traditional guest house in an early Victorian house set
back from the street with veggie proprietor and staff. Close to
Bristol city centre. 2 singles £22.50-£26; 2 doubles £39.50; 1
double en suite £46; 1 twin en suite £48.50; 3 family rooms
£52.50 for 3 people or £42 as a twin. All rooms have central
heating, remote control TV, ioniser, washbasins and tea/coffee
making with herb teas on request. Price includes continental
breakfast of beverages, fruit juice, cereal, warm croissants with
jam and as much toast as you can eat. 5 choices of cooked
veg/vegan brekkers £2-2.50. They have vegan margarine,
soya milk, vegan muesli, veggie sausages. No evening meals
as there are lots of restaurants and take-aways within 2 to 10
minutes walk. Totally non-smoking in public areas. 10% discount to Vegetarian and Vegan Society and PETA members at
weekends.
Directions: M4, M32, right at T junction onto A4044 Bond St.
At roundabout take third exit A38 northwards (Cheltenham
Rd). Go under railway arches and at mini roundabout turn left
into Cotham Brow.

Pushpanjli Indian Vegetarian Restaurant

217A Gloucester Road
Horfield
Bristol
Avon BS7 8NN
Tel: 0117-924 0493 Fax: 0117-924 0493
Open: Mon-Sat 12.30-14.00, 18.30-22.00. Closed Sun.
Excellent Gujarati Indian vegetarian restaurant and take-away
with some East African influences. Most dishes are vegan with
dairy clearly marked. 15 starters £1.95-2.95 with all the usual

such as bhajias, samosas, kachori, bhel puri, idli sambar. Or have a selection of 5 starters for £2.95. Masala dhosa £3.95. Main course thali of dal, two veg curries, basmati rice, one starter, pappadum, salad and a nan £9.45. 12 curries £3.25-3.95 such as aubergine, mixed vegetable (aubergines, courgettes, potatoes, capsicums, peas, stuffed bananas and special dumplings cooked with spices), spinach and lentil, mushroom, black-eyed beans, chick peas, lentil dal. Various breads £1.20-1.50. Brown or white basmati rice £1.85. (How many Indians do you know with brown rice?) Special fried pulao rice £2.25. Children's portions. House wine £7.90 litre, £3.95 half litre, £1.50 glass. Other wines £8.25-12.95, champagne £29.95. Tea and coffee 95p. Soya milk available. Minimum charge £8 during busy periods. Not too far from the Arches Hotel.

Royce Rolls Wholefood Café

The Corn Exchange
St Nicholas Market, Corn St
Bristol
Avon BS1 1JQ
Tel: 0117-982 4228 Fax: 0117-982 4228
Open: Mon-Fri 07.30-16.00, Sat 09.30-16.00. Closed Sun.
Friendly central vegetarian take-away with café seating too. Vegan and gluten free etc available. The name is based on their filled roll which is a special unique recipe with a mix of wholewheat ingredients. Also pastas, savouries, samosas, home-made cakes. Herbal teas 45p, coffee 90p. Soya milk available. No alcohol.

The Rowan Tree

Berkeley Place, The Triangle
Clifton, Bristol, Avon BS8 1EH
Tel: 0117-929 0112
Open: Mon-Sat 9-17.30. Closed Sun.

Lovely wholefood vegetarian café with a patio, close to the city museum and art gallery and the University, offering brilliant value. Plenty for vegans or gluten free. Organic baked beans on toast £1.30, baked potatoes £1.30 with fillings extra, vegan soups of the day £1.60. Salad portions 70p from a rotating selection of 35 such as pasta and olive, wild rice, carrot and seaweed, celery and apple in soyanaise, bulgar wheat. 6 vegan and 3 veggie savouries £1.30-1.85 such as pies, pasties, quiches, bhajias, samosas. Veg and vegan granary bread sandwiches £1.20 take-away, £1.40 eat in. Desserts 60-99p like vegan caropots, trifles, cakes, some wheat or sugar free. 15 herb teas only 65p a pot. Barley cup, Yannoh, dandelion coffee, drinking chocolate, filter coffee 75p-95p. Juices and cordials 70p. Mineral water 60p bottle. No alcohol. 48 seats + 30 outside in good weather. Highchairs for children. Wheelchair access. NUS discount 5%.

Bowlers Restaurant

40 Alfred Place
Kingsdown, Bristol
Avon BS2 8HD
Tel: 0117-924 5026 Fax: 0117-904 0878
Bowlers@Compuserve.Com
Open: every day 11.30-14.30, Tue-Sat evenings
Omnivorous. Organic wholefood. Formerly the award winning vegetarian restaurant Mildred's, this is now Bristol's first organic restaurant registered with the Soil Association. The bad news is that they now serve dead animals, albeit organic ones. So if you don't mind sitting next to someone eating rabbit, deer or squid, you can start with a broccoli soufflé or grilled aubergine with sweet chilli paste, followed by baked butternut squash with sundried tomatoes and walnuts, and finish up with light grapefruit cheesecake, pears in cassis, sticky toffee pudding or bananas in coconut milk. Two courses £11.50, three £14.50. Reservations recommended.

Cornwall

Coverack

The Croft

The Croft
Coverack
Cornwall TR12 6TF
Tel: 01326-280387 Fax: 01326-280387
Open all year

Vegetarian B&B with 1/2 acre garden to the cliff edge. 3 twin en suite rooms with sea views £16.50-22.50 per person. Tea/coffee making in rooms. TV lounge. Veggie and vegan breakfasts including veggie sausages, muesli, soya milk & vegan marg. Evening meal £9 can be vegan on request. Nearby attractions: South West Way, National Trust & S.S.I. protected coastline, Gweek seal sanctuary, Goonhilly Earth Station.
Directions: situated on Lizard Pennisula. From Helston take A3083 Lizard Rd, then turn left onto B3293 for St. Keverna/Coverack. OSRef: SW783187.

Newquay

Treisaac Farm Vegetarian & Vegan Guest House

St Columb Minor
Newquay
Cornwall TR8 4DX
Tel: 01637 880326 Fax:

1 twin en suite, 1 double en suite and 1 without, but has window seat with garden view. Twin £19 pp,£120 weekly, double £21 pp, £133 weekly, dogs welcome £2 per night. 250 year old granite farmhouse with log fire and central heating. 3 course evening meal £11.50 using home grown organic produce where possible. Packed lunches available for day trips. At the end of a secluded lane only 2 miles from the spectacular Cornish coast with some of Britains best beaches. On A3059 between Newquay and A30.

Penzance

Dolphin Cottage

Newtown
Lamorna, St Buryan
Penzance
Cornwall TR19 6BQ
Tel: 01736 810394 Fax:
1 twin, 1 double, 1 single £18 pp, discount for 2 or more nights.

Vegetarian bed and breakfast for women and girls over 12 only, non-smoking, sometimes do an evening meal. The proprietors are healers and artists, some treatments are available such as acupuncture, massage and herbalism. Half mile past turn for Lamorna Cove on B3315 take left to Menwinnion.

Brown's Café

Brown's Gallery
Bread Street
Penzance
Cornwall
Tel: 01736 51302 Fax:
Mon-Sat 10.00-16.00 Closed Sunday

Vegetarian wholefood café, entrees £1.90-£2.75 normally 2 vegan options. Salad bowl/plate £2-£3.00 from 6 variations. 4-5 mains curry, casserole, pasta, pies etc. Desserts 95p-£2.00 cakes, puddings, soya ice cream. House wine £8.00.

Dandelions

39A Causewayhead
Penzance, Cornwall TR18 2ST
Tel: 01736 367683 Fax:
Open: Mon-Sat 9.30-17.00, closed Sun

Vegetarian café with vegan food too.

St Agnes

Porthvean Hotel & Frins Restaurant

Churchtown
St Agnes
Cornwall TR5 0QP
Tel: 01872 552581 Fax:
Open all year.

Three star Hotel, with 7 rooms from £20-£37.50 pp per night, depending on season, discounted for more than one night stay and when you eat in their restaurant. All rooms en suite with remote control t/v, telephone, tea/coffee, heated towel rail, hairdryer etc. Extra bed or cot available for children, under 8 free, 8+ £15 per night. Credit cards accepted. Frin's restaurant, offers a large vegetarian or vegan selection. Veggie pate £2.95, soup £2.55, main course from £6.75, desserts from £2.95.

In the heart of St Agnes village, in what was an inn 200 years ago. Situated in the heart of Poldark country, with the rugged cliffs and coves of North Cornwall. Sandy beach within walking distance, with shop, café and pub. St Agnes is well signposted from the A30,

St Austell

Mount Pleasant Farm

Gorran High Lanes
St Austell
Cornwall PL26 6LR
Tel: 01726 843918 Fax:
1st April to 31st October, 2 double (I en suite) £14-20, 1 family £14-17

Former farmhouse in an acre of ground only a mile from the sea specialising in vegetarian/vegan food. Also an organic smallholding. Evening meal £10, using organic produce wherever possible, gluten free, Hay or raw diets can be catered for. Quiet and peaceful location one mile from coast with it`s famous path. 10% discount for Vegetarian and Vegan card carrying members.Take road from St Austell to Mevagissey, up steep hill past Pentewan beach take right signposted Gorran,

A few miles then a phone box and white house on right. Take next right at cross roads, signposted Mount Pleasant Farm.

St Ives

Woodcote Hotel

The Saltings
Lelant
St Ives
Cornwall TR26 3DL
Tel: 01736-753147 Fax:
Vegetarian hotel 8 rooms/3 en-suite. Open March-October
Established in the early 1920s, the UK's oldest vegetarian hotel. Tea/coffee in rooms, wasbasin, t/v lounge and t/v in en suite rooms. Breakfast vegetarian or vegan. Dinner £13 pre booking only also available to non residents. Relaxed and informal atmosphere overlooking the beautiful tidal estuary of Hayle. Near to seal and RSPB sanctuaries, also arty St Ives.

St Judes Guest House

St Ives Road
Carbis Bay
St Ives, Cornwall TR26 2SF
Tel: 01736 795255 Fax:
Family run vegetarian guesthouse, open all year.
1 single, 2 doubles + 2 en suite, 1 twin + 1 en suite, 2 family rooms. From £15.50-£17.50 pp. Children under 14 half price. Tea/coffee, washbasin, t/v in rooms.
Overlooking St Ives Bay offering accommodation in modern and comfortable surroundings together with a varied whole-food menu. Near Barclay`s bank, in a bungalow, on St Ives Road which runs through Carbis Bay, to the south of St Ives.

Making Waves Vegan Guest House

3 Richmond Place
St Ives
Cornwall TR26 1JN
Tel: 01736 793895 Fax:
2 single £20-£24, 2 double £16-£24, 1 twin £19-£20,1 family
£22.50-£24 pp
Vegan green guesthouse open March-November in picturesque St Ives, tea/coffee and washbasin in rooms. T/v
lounge with books, stereo, guitar etc. very children friendly.
Organic 3 course vegan dinner £12.50 to non residents £9.50
guests. Will collect guests from bus or rail station. Art, sun, sea
and sand abound. 10% discount Vegan Soc. Animal Aid, PETA
and Viva members.

Boswednack Manor & Campion Cottage

Zennor
St Ives
Cornwall TR26 3DD
Tel: 01736 794183 Fax:
1 single £15-£17, 2 double en suite £18-£20 pp, 1 twin £15-
£17, 1 family £15-£17
Spacious granite farmhouse overlooking the magnificent
Gurnard's Head offering b&b and vegetarian evening meal £9,
no t/v, does have meditation room and also offers courses on
archaeology and painting throughout the year. Also Campion
Cottage a 17th century farm building which sleeps 5, from
£170pw-£320 in high season. Area of outstanding natural
beauty rich in wildlife. 1 mile west of Zennor on B3306 St Ives
to Lands End road.

The Cafe

Island Square
St. Ives
Cornwall
Tel: 01736 793621 Fax:

Vegetarian restaurant. Main courses include cashew nut koftas with fresh mango sauce & couscous; oriental aubergines with black bean sauce and stir fry noddles. Desserts include lemon & almond tart, chocolate amaretto torte. Beer £1.40, house wine £6.80, £1.70 glass. Teas 70p, coffee 90p. 20 seats. Children's portions available.

Tintagel

Trevarvan House

Trewarmett
Tintagel
Cornwall PL34 0ES
Tel: 01840 770486 Fax:
Small family guest house £14 pp, £94 weekly with sea views from all rooms.
Vegetarian, vegan, allergen free and special diets catered for. Tea/coffee and baby listening facility available. In an outstanding position with spectacular view towards Trebarwith Strand and 20 miles of coastline. Sandy beach and some of the highest cliffs in Cornwall. Popular with surfers and sunbathers. In midst of "King Arthur Country", Tintagel, Merlins Cave, Slaughter Bridge all nearby. Coastal footpath for walkers. On B3263 just over a mile from Tintagel.

Michael House

Trelake Lane
Treknow
Nr Tintagel
Cornwall PL34 0EW
Tel: 01840 770592 Fax:
Michaelhse @ AOL.COM
2 double £15-50-£18-50 + 1 en suite £20-£22.50, 1 twin £18.50, 1 family £17.50
Vegetarian guest house and restaurant in local slate and stone

house with sea views from most rooms. 10 minute walk to Trebarwith Strand a popular beach for families and surfers (equipment and bicycles hired daily). In the heart of Cornish King Arthur country (maybe he went to Glastonbury for his holidays). Lovely walk to Tintagel Castle and Merlins Cave also Bodmin Moors a little further afield. 3 course set dinner £10 with vegan choice. Packed lunches and pasties always available. From A39 1 mile south of Tintagel, from Bude to Wadebridge Road take B3263 (Camelford-Tintagel) until Trewarmett, as you go through village a small garden centre on left followed by a left hand bend on brow of hill. Immediately following the corner is an unmarked lane on left. This leads into Treknow. Michael House is on the right just before the church, ample parking.

Mystery Veggie Guest House

Nr Tintagel
Cornwall
Tel: 01840 770944 Fax:
1 double and 1 twin £12 pp Easter-September.
Small guest house that will only accept prebookings, please phone for details.

Truro

The Feast

15 Kenwyn Street
Truro
Cornwall TR1 3BU
Tel: 01872 72546 Fax:
Mon-Sat 10-17.00 closed Sun. Last weekend of month open for themed evening.
Vegetarian world food restaurant with good choice of Belgian fruit, white, blonde and chimay beers. Starters £1.55-£2.70 4 vegan. Salads £2.50-£3.40, savoury & sweet pancakes, jacket potatoes, sandwiches, dish of day etc. Desserts feature enticing ice creams, cakes made on premises. The Belgians have a well deserved reputation for the most enjoyable cakes, do leave space for one.

Devon

Ashburton

Cuddyford

Rew Road
Ashburton
Devon TQ13 7EN
Tel: 01364 653325 Fax: 01364 653325
1x double £15-£18; 1x twin £15-£18; (can make double into

family room)
Vegetarian and vegan b&b in deepest Devon. Situated in a rural setting within Dartmoor National Park and 3 course evening meal £10 featuring wholesome cookery with local produce. Local attractions include white water sports on Dart, sailing, beaches, walking, steam trains, nearby sports hall with gym and of course Dartmoor. Take A38 to Ashburton, down main street to Golden Lion opposite which is Roborough Lane, after a half mile take left at cross road into Rew Road, Cuddyford is 4th house on right.

Chard

Rastra Devas

Holmbush
Thorncombe
Chard
Devon TA20 4PL
Tel: 0127 678597 Fax:
2 doubles £30 each includes 4 course dinner, courses or retreats. Daily and non-residential courses £25/day.
Vegan and no deceased animal or dodgy dairy products allowed in. Small cottage run by healers, herbalism, iridology, reiki, meditation, aromatherapy, stress management etc, with self-catering accommodation for up to 10 people in the grounds, though they provide breakfast, lunch, tea and big dinner anyway. Beds are provided but to keep costs down they ask you to bring towels and bedding or sleeping bag.

Dartington

Cranks

Cider Press Centre
Shinners Bridge
Dartington
Devon TQ9 6JB
Tel: 01803 862 388 Fax:
Mon-Sat 9.30-17.00 also Sundays from Easter-December.
Branch of the famous veggie chain of restaurants in amongst lots of arty-crafty shops. Very nice for a day out.

Herbies

15 North Street
Exeter
Devon EX4 3QS
Tel: 01392 258473 Fax:
Open Mon1100-1430;Tue-Fri 1100-1430 and 1800-2130;Sat 1030-1600 and 1800-2130. Closed Sunday. Vegetarian café and restaurant, starters £2.20-£2.95 dhal, pate, houmos, guacamole etc. Snacks £2.05-£3.65 nut & beanburgers, pizza, stir fry, jacket potatoes and stuffed pitta breads. Mains nut roast, chillie, curry, lasagne, flan, pie etc. Good selection of desserts with imaginative vegan choices. Very interesting wine, beer and spirits.

Ilfracombe

The Angel Diner

23 Church Street
Ilfracombe
Devon EX34 8HB
Tel: 01271 866 833 Fax:
19.00-22.30 everyday.
Offers 6-7 vegetarian dishes.

Lynton

Bear Hotel

Lydiate Lane
Lynton
Devon EX34 6AJ
Tel: 01598 753391 Fax:
A high standard of accommodation is offered in this ETB 3 crown Georgian hotel. 9 rooms, all en suite, including 2 singles, 1 triple, 1 family room with 2 doubles and a single, and 5 double rooms. £20-27 per person. Some rooms have sofas. Three course evening meal £13 in their omnivorous restaurant

with good veggie food. Vegans will need to warn them as it's only a small hotel with one cook.

Newton Abbot

The Country Table

12 Bank Street
Newton Abbot
Devon
Tel: 01626 202 120 Fax:
Mon-Sat 9.00-17.50 Closed Sunday
Healthy wholefood veggie café, restaurant and take-away. Breakfasts, fry up £3.15, Saturdays only. Soups £2.20, salads £1.75-£2.75, sandwiches £2.30-£2.70 also double decker baguettes. Mains £3.75 spicy parsnip & lentil pie, bean & tomato bake, wild mushroom lasagne. Scones, cakes and afternoon tea, desserts £2.25. Tea, coffee, soya milkshakes etc. 10% discount to Vegetarian & Vegan Society members.

Okehampton

The Sanctuary

The Sanctuary
Nr Lydford
Okehampton
Devon EX20 4AL
Tel: 01822 820203 Fax:
1 single, 1 double, 1 twin £10pp or £49 per week.
Vegan b&b in house used as Vegfam headquarters, all profits go to the charity. Very peaceful location with Dartmoor and all it's delights on doorstep. On A386 Lydford at T junction where road crosses the Lyd, in middle of S bend. You need to book so check directions then.

The Sandpiper Vegetarian Hotel

14 Roundham Rd
Paignton, Devon TQ4 6DN
Tel: 01803 551397 Fax: 01803 551397
4 singles (2 en suite) £18-£22, 7 double (4 en suite) & 3 twin (1 en suite) £18-£22, also 2 family rooms £55-£70. All rooms with tea/coffee and t/v. Guest lounge and bar. 3 course vegetarian or vegan dinner £13.50 special diets can be catered for. 5% discount for Veg & Vegan Soc. members, also 7 nights plus discount. In heart of English Riviera between the picturesque harbour and Goodrington sands. Lovely coastal walk to Brixham. Second turning on right after harbour, courtesy service from rail station.

Heart & Soul

37 New Street
The Barbican
Plymouth
Devon PL1 2NA
Tel: 01752-263590/255835 Fax:
Mon-Sat 10.00-17.00 closed Sun
Vegetarian café recommended by Plymouth reader who says they also do vegan food. No details sent from them so it's pot luck. When we get a menu we`ll give more info.

Plymouth Arts Centre Vegetarian Restaurant

Plymouth Arts Centre
38 Looe Street
Plymouth, Devon PL4 0EB
Tel: 01752 202616 Fax:

Mon 10-17.00, Tu 10-21.00, Wed 10-20.00, Th 10-21.00, Fr-Sat 10-20.00 Sun 18-20
Café offering entrees 80p-£1.60, soup, pate. Salads 65p each. Main £1-£3.50 at least two vegan aubergine & pistachio pie, curry lentil fritter, homity pie, jacket potato. Desserts £1-£1.60 crumbles, trifle, treacle tart etc.

The Caffeine Club

45 Tavistock Place
Plymouth, Devon PL4 8AX
Tel: 01752-262620 Fax:
Open: Mon-Fri 9-24.00, Sat 11-24.00, Sun 11-22.00
Brand new vegetarian coffee house in the centre of town which has restaurant food in the evenings and is looking at specializing in vegan food.

Veggie Perrin's

97 Mayflower Street
Plymouth
Devon
Tel: 01752 252 888 Fax: 01752 220808
Mon-Sat 12.00-14.30, 17.00-22.00, closed Sun except for bookings.
Gujarati vegetarian cuisine restaurant and takeaway. Starters £1.20-£2.40 samosa, bhaji, kachori, stuffed puri etc. Squillions of veg curries £2.90-£4.95, various paneers and "korma sutra". Beans, pulses and dhals. Rice from £1.50 and all those scrummy breads, also that English ethnic delicacy, chips. Various desserts (only one vegan), big selection of Indian and world beers. As much as you like buffet, lunch time £4.50 and Monday night £5.50. Also takeaway, about 20% less than quoted prices.

Tooleys

The Ridgeway
Plympton
Devon
Tel: 01752-342211 Fax:
Open Wed-Mon 17.30-23.30, closed Tue
Chinese take-away with a separate vegetarian menu containing 57 dishes under £3.50 and 2 set menus for two people £10-11. The cook is a pure Buddhist. During the day it's an ordinary café.

Sidmouth

Enstone Guest House

Lennox Avenue
Sidmouth
Devon EX10 8TX
Tel: 01395 514444 Fax:
April to September 3 double, 1 double, 1 family £14.50-£21.50
Traditional Guest House with vegetarian proprietor, small & friendly, adjacent to the river Sid and a few minutes walk to the town centre and esplanade. Veggie breakfast and 4 course evening meal only £7. 10% discount for Vegetarian Soc. Members.

Slapton near Kingsbridge

The Roundhouse

Slapton near Kingsbridge
Devon TQ7 2PN
Tel: 01548 580019 Fax:
1 double and 1 family room £16-£18 pp
Vegetarian proprietors offer accommodation in this listed 18th century house in the centre of the village of Slapton opposite church. Local attractions include Slapton Ley nature reserve.

Torquay

Brookesby Hall Hotel

Hesketh Road
Torquay
Devon TQ1 2LN
Tel: 01803 292194 Fax:
3 single £17.50-£19.50, 5 double £35-£44 2 en suite, 2 twin
£35-£41, 1 family.
Vegetarian hotel in elegant Victorian villa with large suntrap gardens overlooking Torbay. Tea coffee in rooms, t/v lounge, vegetarian or vegan 3 course evening meal £13.50, also available to non residents. 10% discount for 7 day or more bookings to card carrying Veg & Vegan Soc. Members.

Totnes

The Brioche Wholefood Coffee Shop

49 Fore Street
Totnes, Devon
Tel: 01803-864463 Fax:
Open: Mon-Sat 9-16.45, last food orders 15.30, closed Sun
Vegetarian café. Vegans can have hummous or baked beans.

Tolivers

67 Fore Street
Totnes, Devon TQ9 5NJ
Tel: 01803-862604 Fax:
Open: Mon-Sat 10-17.00, also Fri-Sat and most Thu 19-23.00.
Summer Sun 10-18.00
Vegetarian café. They have some vegan dishes, including a couple in the evening, and if you don't like them then they'll knock up a stir-fry.

Willow Vegetarian Garden Restaurant

87 High Street
Totnes
Devon TQ9 5PB
Tel: 01803 862 605 Fax:
Mon-Tue 10.00-17.00, Wed-Sat 10.00-17.00 & 19.00-23.00
Closed Sun
Vegetarian wholefood restaurant using organic produce where available. Large Vegan selection. Starters £1.10-£2.75 lunchtime £1.75-£2.95 evenings celery & cashew soup, basil & tofu dip, pakoras. 3 salads £1.30-£5.95 when as main course. Frijoles con salsa, Irish stew with dumplings (veggie of course), brocolli & tofu in peanut sauce, Alsace onion tart £3.10-£4.95. Desserts 95p-£3.50 toffee hunzas, chocolate forest, meringue utang which sounds great. Also cakes, ice cream etc. Superb selection of organic beers, lager & cider, also 9 wines of which 8 are vegan from £6.80 a bottle. On Wednesday evenings there is an Indian night featuring the old favourites such as thali`s and some interesting Indian regional foods. Highly recommended to us by local vegetarians.

Dorset

Bournemouth

St. Antoine

2 Guildhill Rd
Southbourne
Bournemouth
Dorset BH6 3EY
Tel: 01202 433043 Fax:
Omnivorous guest house with vegetarian staff which has catered for veggies and vegans for 13 years. Veggie dishes are homemade using separate utensils and home grown vegetables where possible, so there'll be no problem checking out the ingredients. 1 single room £17-20, 2 doubles £18-21per person, 2 twins £18-21, 2 family rooms en suite £18-21. Tea/coffee making and washbasins but not TV in rooms. TV

lounge. Full English veggie or vegan breakfasts with vegan soya milk, muesli and marg. Evening meal for residents only £8. e.g. home made soup or pate, curried stuffed mushrooms with rice or veg, homemade apple and cranberry pie, tea or coffee. 5 minutes walk from the beach and river 5 mins. Tennis and bowls 100 yards away. No smoking in rooms.

The Salad Centre

667 Christchurch Road
Bournemouth
Dorset BH7 6AA
Tel: 01202 393 673 Fax:
Mon-Sat 10.00-17.00 closed Sun
Vegetarian wholefood restaurant and take away in fun and funky Bournemouth, great beach and lots of Euros in Summer. Soups, hoummous etc. £1.40-£2.15, 30 salads £2.35-£3.95. Jacket potatoes, pizza, nut roast, homity pie, bakes, casseroles and daily specials £2.95-£3.95. Various desserts with 20 odd vegan cakes and an aftenoon tea tray £3.25. Also a 5% discount to Vegetarian and Vegan Soc. and Animal Aid members.

Lyme Regis

Firleas

8 Colway Close
Lyme Regis
Dorset DT7 3BE
Tel: 01297 443528 Fax:
Vegetarian guest house in a chalet bungalow overlooking gardens and sea providing a relaxed atmosphere for visitors. One twin and one single £15.50 per person. Dinner by arrangement, 2 courses with coffee/tea £8. Organic produce and home baking feature at mealtimes. Vegan food no problem, soya milk or nut milk.

Poole

Clipper Restaurant

The Dolphin Centre
Poole
Dorset
Tel: 01202 683334 Fax:
Open: Mon-Fri 9.30-16.45, Sat 9-19.00, closed Sun
Veg section of non veg café recommended by local veggies, though there isn't much for vegans. At the top of the shopping centre, next to Beales department store.

Swanage

Seashells Hotel

7 Burlington Road
Swanage
Dorset BH19 1LR
Tel: 01929 422794 Fax:
2 single, 2 double, 1 twin, 3 family all en suite £18-£34 + 1
family flat
Vegetarian hotel overlooking Swanage Bay with t/v, tea coffee in all rooms. 4 course evening meal £12, vegans catered for, also wide choice of beers, organic wine and non alchoholic drinks. Opposite a safe sandy beach, 1 min walk, beach huts can be hired for that quintessential English experience, for any foreign readers it is a little wooden hut with a kettle and small stove, usually with a "jokey" name, that you can only use during the day. Great walking country, the Dorset coastal path and the Purbeck Hills. Sailing, windsurfing, canoeing and boat trips, also a fitness club with sauna and heated pool nearby. From Bournemouth ferry follow road to Swanage, past modern church take 2nd road on left. Or from seafront turn left then 2nd turn on right.

Westbourne

Flossies

73 Seamoor Road
Westbourne
Dorset
Tel: 01202 769 959 Fax:
Mon-Sat 9.00-17.00 closed Sunday
Vegetarian.

Wimborne

Formosa

81 Wimborne Road
East End, Corfe Mullen
Wimborne
Dorset BH21 3DS
Tel: 01202 887323 Fax:
Fresh and filling breakfasts are offered in this friendly vegetarian family home only a mile from Wimborne. One family room with a double and a single bed plus a travel cot, £16 per person. No evening meal, but there are pubs nearby and other places with veggie food. Handy for the Poole-Cherbourg ferry. Directions: on the Wimborne Rd that crosses the A31 Corfe Mullen Road.

Somerset

Bridgwater

The Cycle Inn

101 St John St
Bridgwater
Somerset TA6 5HX
Tel: 01278 421099 Fax:
Mon-Sat 11.00-23.00, Sun 11.00-22.30

Vegetarian, organic in delightful Bridgewater. Starters £1.50-£1.95 tapenade, broccoli & stilton soup. Mains £3.95-£5.95 bean casserole, courgette & mushroom bolognese, creamy vegetables all served with bulgar salad, coleslaw and green salad. Desserts £1.95 raisin & nut tart with spicey pastry, fruit crumble.House wine £6.99 bottle.

Poplar Herb Farm
Burtle
Bridgwater
Somerset TA7 8NB
Tel: 01278 723170 Fax:
Vegetarian bed and cooked breakfast on an organic herb farm using much of its own organic vegetables fruit and to provide exclusively vegetarian meals. One double room and a family room with a double and single bed, £14 per person. Another double en suite £17 per person. Evening meal £9.50. Friendly rescued donkeys, goats and cats.

Parsonage Farm
Over Stowey
Bridgwater
Somerset TA5 1HA
Tel: 01278 733237 Fax:
Vegetarian traditional farmhouse. 1 double £18 pp, Double en suite £21 pp, Single £25. 3 course evening meal, light supper £7. 17th century with log fires, set in walled gardens, ideally located for the Quantock Hills. Vegetarian owners offer home cooked meals using produce from their own organic smallholding.

Merefield Vegetarian Guest House

East Street
Crewkerne
Somerset TA18 7AB
Tel: 01460 73112 Fax:
1 double £17.50 + 1 en suite £22.50, 1 twin £19
16th century listed building of historic interest, with walled south facing gardens. All the rooms have tea/coffee, radio and hairdryer. Large drawing room with games, books and videos. 3 course vegetarian dinner prepared by vegan owner for £8.50 which includes a complimentary jug of the local cider, wonderful stuff. For walkers, direct access to the countryside is reached through the paddock, the sunken lane is part of a designated nature trail. Crewkerne has a rail station and a pick up can be arranged.

Exford

Exmoor Lodge

Chapel Street
Exford
Somerset TA24 7PY
Tel: 01643 831694 Fax:
1 single £15, 3 double 2 en suite £30-£42, 1 twin en suite £38
Vegetarian guest house overlooking the village green in the centre of the village of Exford in the heart of the Exmoor National Park. Dinner for £12 is normally vegan, gluten free or food allergy diets can be caterered for by the Cordon Vert qualified proprietor. Porlock, Dunster, Lynton and Dulverton nearby, walking, cycling or horseriding on the moor or sitting to watch the deer, birds or Exmoor ponies should relax even the most stressed visitor. 10% discount for 5 plus nights. From M5 junction 23 take A39 towards Minehead, take left at traffic lights on to A396 and continue to Wheddon Cross, then turn rght to Exford on B3224, the Lodge is in the village centre overlooking the green.

Ramala Centre

The Old Stables. Chalice Hill House
Dod Lane
Glastonbury
Somerset BA6 8BZ
Tel: 01458 832459 Fax:

Vegetarian bed and breakfast. This universal spiritual centre encompassing all religions, welcomes all to the Grade II listed Georgian Manor House set amongst beautiful gardens in the heart of Glastonbury, just off the High Street. One double £25 per person, one twin en suite £30 each. No evening meal but you won't starve in the town. OK for vegans.

Rosemullion

The Kingfisher Centre
54 Roman Way
Glastonbury
Somerset BA6 8AD
Tel: 01458 831182 Fax:
4 Double 1 Single

Completely vegan guest house with 2 doubles, 2 twins (can be used as singles) and one single room, £20 per person. All rooms have washbasins. Evening meal around £7. Beautiful garden.

Brock Cottage

77 Bere Lane
Glastonbury
Somerset BA6 8BE
Tel: 01458 834985 Fax:
Open all year.

Vegetarian B&B. One single en suite with own entrance £20-25. One twin with view of Glastonbury Abbey and one double

£17.50-22.00. Tea/coffee making in all rooms. TV lounge. Full English veggie and vegan breakfasts. No evening meal. 10% discount to members of Vegetarian and Vegan Societies and Animal Aid. Close to many vegetarian restaurants and Wookey Hole.

Directions: On A361 opposite the Rural Life Museum.

Waterfall Cottage

20 Old Wells Rd
Glastonbury
Somerset BA6 8ED
Tel: 01458 831707 Fax:
1 single, 1 twin £14.50-£!6
Vegetarian run b&b in 17th century cottage with views of Tor. Also therapies available to help you unwind. Few minutes walk from town with all it`s attractions and eateries. The Abbey gardens with King Arthurs grave, mystical Glastonbury Tor, Chalice Well garden with the holy grail legend, Wearyall Hill with Joseph of Arimathea`s tree, Vale of Avalon etc. Do feel free to tell locals you thought King Arthur lived in Cornwall. Nearby attractions are Avebury, Wells, Cheddar Gorge, Wells (smallest city) and just 15 miles to Somerset coast. From town centre take High St up the hill then Boveton to Old Wells Road. Glastonbury is reached by either A39 or A361.

Cafe Galatea

5a High Street
Glastonbury
Somerset BA6 9DP
Tel: 01458 834 284 Fax:
Open: Sun 11-9pm, Mon -4pm, Tue -6pm, Wed -9opm, Thu/Fri -10pm, Sat 10.30-10pm.
Very nice vegetarian and vegan café.

Rainbows End Cafe

17a High Street
Glastonbury
Somerset BA6 9DP
Tel: 01458 833 896 Fax:
Mon-Fri 10.00-16.00, Fri-Sat 10.00-16.30, Sun 11.00-16.00
Lunchtime café in downtown Glastonbury, Starters £1.50-£3.00 soups, quiches, houmous. Five speciality salads available daily, £2.00. Mains £3-3.50 sweet potatoes & roast red peppers, cheese & spinach pie. Desserts £2.00. House wine £6 bottle.

Porloch

Seapoint

Seapoint, Upway
Porloch, Somerset TA24 8QE
Tel: 01643 862289 Fax: 01643 862289
Open Feb- Nov inclusive. Winter breaks available between Nov-Feb

Omnivorous Edwardian guest house with a roaring fire on chilly evenings in the lounge, set in Exmoor National Park, overlooking the ocean. Wonderful walking and wildlife, especially red deer. 2 days dinner, B&B for £49 p.p. Three rooms available - two double en suite, and one twin en suite. £21 p.p. for all rooms. No single supplements. TV, washbasins, and tea/coffee making in rooms, plus TV lounge. £12.50 for evening meal e.g. home made soup with rolls; sweet and sour tofu with cashews rice and salad; apple and raisin pancakes. Vegetarian and vegan wines. Although the establishment is not exclusively vegetarian, the family who runs it is (apart from Dad!), thus all approprite vegetarian breakfast essentials are there, and vegans need not worry as a vegan breakfast is available including vegan marg and soya milk.

Located behind the Ship Inn in case you can't do without your beer or G&T. Directions: From A39 West continue through village, veer left at McCoys Saddlery, then left again after the Ship Inn and see private driveway on the left.

The Herb Garden

24 Upper High Street
Taunton
Somerset TA1 3PZ
Tel: 01823-282884 Fax: 01823-353672
Open: Tue 12-15.00. Wed-Sat 12-22.00. Closed Sun-Mon.
Vegetarian and 80% vegan wholefood daytime cafe, takeaway and evening restaurant. Veggie burgers £2.00, falafel £3.50 or £3.90 with humous. Filled rolls £1.50. All day breakfast with tea or coffee £3.20. 4 vegan starters include Oriental mushrooms £2.50, soup of the day £2.50. Four vegan salads £1.50-3.50 such as beetroot and wakame; curried chick pea. 3 vegan and 2 veggie main meals include pasta in baked pepper sauce; ginger and chick pea filo pie; blackeye bean, tomato and rosemary pie; North Indian stuffed aubergine. 4 vegan desserts £1.25-2.50 such as deep dish treacle tart, hot fruit crumble, Swedish glace ice cream. Also cakes and fruit/seed bars from 50p. Large selection of teas, freshly ground coffees, soft drinks, vegan lassi. All wines are vegan and organic, from £7 bottle, £1.80 glass. Beers and ciders include a Scottish vegan organic bitter. Day time counter service and evening table service from 7pm. Wheelchair access. Non-smoking. Highchairs and children's portions. 10% discount to Vegan and Vegetarian Society members.

Nut Tree Farm

Stoughton Cross
Wedmore
Somerset BS28 4QP
Tel: 01934 712404 Fax:
Open all year except Christmas & Boxing Day
Omnivorous period farmhouse set in 2 acres, in the middle of the peaceful Somerset countryside within easy reach of Cheddar Gorge, Wookey Hole and Glastonbury. 1 single en suite £19.50, 1 double and 1 twin both en suite £39, tea/coffee

making in rooms, TV lounge. Also self catering cottage adjoining farmhouse with two bedrooms £165-318 per week. Staff all vegetarian. Offering vegan, vegetarian or wholefood traditional breakfasts, no evening meal. Leave M5 at junction 22, take A38 nort towards Bristol 5 miles to Weare, take right to Wedmore, follow signs for Ashton windmill, then I kilometer is the farm on right.

The Good Earth

4 Priory Road
Wells, Somerset
Tel: 01749 678600 Fax:
Mon-Sat 9.30-17.30 closed Sunday.
Licensed vegetarian restaurant and take away in wholefood store. Soups £1.10-£1.80 leek & potatoe, tomato, onion. Quiche, pizza, jacket potatoe £1.65-£2.25. Choice of salads, mains £2.65 pasta, casserole, nut roast, moussaka etc. Dessert £1.75

Wiltshire

Marlborough

Stones In Marlborough

5 Old Hughenden Yard
Marlborough
Wiltshire SN8 1LT
Tel: 01672-515200 Fax: 01672-515200
Open: Mon-Sat 8.30-17.00
Brand new vegetarian café and coffee bar with food similar to Stones in Avebury, with some new features, including a range of sandwiches for eat in or take-away, espresso and cappuccino coffees. Hot lunch £5.95, hot tart and salad £4.75, sandwiches £3.45-4.25, salads £3.50. Good range of organic and vegetarian wines, beers and ciders. House wine from £8.95 per bottle, £2.25 glass. Teas £1.35 pot. Soya milk available. Children's portions, 1 high chair.

Stones Restaurant

Avebury
Marlborough
Wiltshire SN8 1RF
Tel: 01672-539 514 Fax: 01672-539 683
Open: April-Oct every day 10-18.00; Nov-Mar weekends only 10-17.00; Closed Jan.
Vegetarian restaurant in a 19th century stable block built of the same sarsen stone as the adjacent megalithic stone circle. Menu changes daily with always 2 hot lunches, 5 different salads and several cold savouries. In 14 years owners Michael and Hilary Howard, both trained archaeologists and formerly in charge of Avebury museum, have never served the same dish twice and the food is so good that most of the regulars aren't even vegetarian. They grow their own vegetables, herbs and salad leaves "not simply because we felt strongly about lorry mileage, cold storage and so on, but because the flavour is simply incomparable." Witness up to 1,000 customer a day in

summer queuing for gourmet vegetarian food from all over the world at bargain prices freshy prepared with nothing frozen or reheated. Lunch £5.95, salad £2.95, soup £2.95, savoury £2.50. House wine £8.95 bottle, £2.25 glass. The have French organic wine, Hugh Rock's range of English country wines, Dunkertons cider and beer from the local old-fashioned brewery. Teas £1.10 pot, coffee 90p-£1.10. Soya milk available. 3 highchairs. Wheelchair access.

Recipe book Stones Spells for Magic Feasts by Hilary Howard, Digging Deep, £17.95.

SOUTH EAST ENGLAND

EAST SUSSEX

Bexhill on Sea

Corianders

66 Devonshire Road
Bexhill on Sea
East Sussex TN40 1AX
Tel: 01424 220 329 Fax:
Open: Mon-Sat 9-17.00
Omnivorous restaurant with one vegetarian and one vegan
dish daily, £2-3. Jacket potatoes £1.30, £2.10 with filling.
Salads 95p, £1.50, £1.75. Vegan and wheatfree homemade
cakes. Almost on the seafront, near the car park.

Brighton

Rozanne Mendick

14 Chatsworth Road
Brighton
East Sussex BN1 5DB
Tel: 01273 556584 Fax:
SMMARKS@fastnet.co.uk
Vegetarian B&B with 1 single and one twin room, £17.50 per
person.
Large family home 20 minutes walk from the seafront, pier,
pavillion and town centre, offering vegetarian and vegan bed
and breakfast with full English or continental options including
vegan marg. and muesli, veggie sausages etc and soya milk.
Tea/coffee making and TV in rooms.
Directions: 10 minutes walk from Brighton train station. At the
junction of Dyke Road and The Old Shoreham Road.

Paskins Town House Hotel

18/19 Charlotte St
Brighton
East Sussex BN2 1AG
Tel: 01273-601203 Fax: 01273-621 973
welcome@paskins.co.uk
Open 365 days

Omnivorous hotel with vegetarian proprietor, 10 minutes walk East from the pier in a quiet street off Marine Parade. Paskins promises you a stay that will evoke memories of a more gracious age. Most of the individually designed rooms have en suite facilities, colour TV, direct dial phone and most have trouser presses. For an added touch of luxury treat yourself to a four poster bed. 1 single £20, 6 en suite £30. 1 double £40, 8 en suite £60, with four poster £70. 1 twin £40, 2 en suite £60. Children up to 11 sharing with 2 adults pay 75%. Enquire about special weekend rates. Full English or continental veggie or vegan breakfast with fruits, compote, juices, cereals followed by something cooked which might include tarragon and sun dried tomato sausages or nut, seed and spice fritters. Tea/coffee, washbasins and TV in rooms. Lounge bar. 10% discount to VSUK and Vegan Society. Loads of vegetarian restaurants within walking distance plus the full monty beach.

The Granville Hotel

124 Kings Rd
Brighton
East Sussex BN1 2FA
Tel: 01273-326302 Fax: 01273-728294
granville@brighton.co.uk
Open all year

Luxurious omnivorous hotel that takes good care of veggies and vegans, right on the sea front in the town centre, close to cafés and restaurants and all of Brighton's entertainments. If you want to spoil yourselves, this is the place for a Brighton weekend! 4 singles ensuite £49-55. 17 doubles ensuite £55-135 with jacuzzis, four posters, water beds. 2 twins ensuite £55-65. One family room £85-105. Tea/coffee making and TV in rooms. Some have sea views. Breakfast in rooms with veggie sausages, soya milk etc. Evening meal £15.50 at Trogs restaurant, open to non-residents, see separate entry.

Bombay Aloo

39 Ship Street
(opposite Post Office)
Brighton
East Sussex BN1 1AB
Tel: 01273 776038 Fax:
Open every day 12-24.00

Vegetarian Indian restaurant with free delivery service. What makes Bombay Aloo unique is that it's 100% vegetarian and vegan with no menu, just one delicious set meal with 14 items for only £4.95.   By serving only 14 dishes, they can maintain freshness throughout at a reasonable price. Set meal for one includes a starter of onion bhajee, somosa and pakora. Main course is six different curries: tarka dal, mixed veg, chick pea aloo, saag and mushroom, veg dansak and peas & aloo. Plus rice, nan bread and fresh salad, with keer and gulab jamun for dessert. Delivery times only 17.30-23.30, minimum order two set meals for free delivery. Delivery hotline free call 0800-393 571.

Food For Friends

17a-18 Prince Albert Street
The Lanes
Brighton
East Sussex BN1 1HF
Tel: 01273 202310 Fax: 01273 775841

Open: Mon-Sat 08.00-22.00, Sun 9.15-22.00
Vegetarian restaurant with some vegan dishes offering global cuisine from a menu that changes daily. Starters could be butterbean, carrot and fresh coriander soup or field mushroom soup £1.45, with organic bread £1.85. Salads £1.80-3.15. Examples of main courses are black eye bean and mushroom korma with rice £2.95; courgette and potato lattice served with a rich tomato and red wine sauce and salad garnish £3.35; Chinese stir fry with rice £3.45; falafel with rice and salad £3.35. Puddings and cakes £1.50 such as vegan summer fruit and nutmeg pie with cream.
House wine £5.95, glass £1.95. Tea 70p, coffee 80p, soya milk and milkshakes. 20% discount to VegSoc, VeganSoc and Viva!

Food For Thought
16 Kensington Gardens
Brighton
East Sussex
Tel: 01273 674 919 Fax:
Open: Mon-Sat 9-17.30. Sometimes open Sun.
Almost completely vegetarian café (apart from 2 dishes).

Terre a Terre
71 East St, Brighton
East Sussex BN1 1NJ
Tel: 01273 729 051 Fax:
Mon 18.00-22.30, Tues-Sun 12.00-22.30
Very popular vegetarian restaurant, very enticing menu, booking recommended. Nibbles 80p roast mixed seeds, herb dried tomatoes. £1.10 olives, marinated tofu. Focaccia £1.75-£2.50. Starters £2.90-£4.75 soup, sushi, borjak pillows, poke mole, plenty of vegan options. Mains £7.75-£8 artichoke rotollo, split pea pikelet. Wide selection of salads from £2.75. Puddings £4.25 only one vegan option. Good freshly cooked food.

The Prince George

The Prince George
5 Trafalgar St
Brighton
East Sussex
Tel: 01273-681055 Fax:
Open: Mon-Thu 12-20.30, Fri-Sun 12-19.00

Vegetarian pub with all types of food at good prices. Start with a soup of the day £1.30-2.50 which could be vegetable pesto soup or spicy Thai lentil. Salads £1-£3.50 could be tomato, Waldorf, Greek etc. Mains £2-£5 such as super holly burgers, roast Mediterranean veg & cous-cous, Thai red curry, penne with fresh pesto and sun-dried tomatoes. No desserts at time of publication but a new menu is on the way. Of course they have beer, house wine £8.50 or £2 glass, tea, coffee, soya milk and soya milkshakes. Discount for members of the Vegetarian or Vegan Society and Brighton based Viva!

Trogs Gourmet Vegetarian Restaurant & Café Bar

124 Kings Road
Brighton
East Sussex BN1 2FA
Tel: 01273 326302 Fax: 01273 728294
Open every day: café bar 12-14, 18-21.30; restaurant 18-21.30

Vegetarian restaurant in the luxurious Granville Hotel on the seafront, serving organic gourmet vegetarian food. They have a separate vegan menu. Four courses for £15.50 with at least four dishes to choose from for each course. Starters could be blood orange and fresh garlic Vichyssoise with crusty bread; roulade; harlequin terrine with a lime and coriander sauce. After an intermezzo sorbet, follow with wild mushroom darioles with a Morel sauce on a bed of asparagus; medley of green vegetables served in a puff pastry feuilletée; leek, almond and tarragon Mousseline dressed with an apricot sauce. All main courses served with a selection of fresh market vegetables, cooked al dente or a little more if you ask. Finish off with white and dark chocolate terrine with a hot fudge sauce. House wine £8.50, £1.75 glass, and there's a fine selection of organic wines. Tea 95p. Cafeteria of coffee with nibbles £1.50. Soya milk and milkshakes, beer. 10% service charge. 10% discount for VSUK, Vegan Society, PeTA, Animal Aid.

Brighton Unemployed Centre Families Project

6 Tilbury Place
Brighton
East Sussex BN2 2GY
Tel: 01273 671213 Fax: 01273 676471
Cafe. Vegan. One meal served per day at 1pm. Cost is £1 for adults and 30p for children. Tea 10-20p, coffee 20p. Deserts occasionally available and may be vegetarian or vegan. Open 10am-4pm Mon-Fri. Closed Sat and Sun. Non-smoking. 50 seats, 3 highchairs available for children. No wheelchair access. No alcohol allowed on premises.

Snookie's

29 Tidy Street, Brighton
East Sussex BN1 4EL
Tel: 01273-677712 Fax: 01273-677712
Open: Mon-Sat 12-15.00 & 17-22.00, Sun 12-18.00
Omnivorous café with separate veggie menu including nut roast £4.25, Spicey Algerian stew, Walnut & green lentil roast.

Vegetarian Shoes

12 Gardner Street
Brighton
East Sussex BN1 1UP
Tel: 01273-691913 Fax:
Doc Martens walking boots, steel toe-capped walking boots, sandals, men's and women's shoes, jackets and belts that look and feel like leather but are made from synthetic materials. Mail order catalogue too. Heaps of other great shops in this area.

Fairwarp

Primrose Patch

Fairwarp
near Uckfield
East Sussex TN22 3BY
Tel: 01825 712097 Fax: 01825 712097
j.masters@mcmail.com
Closed Christmas

Vegetarian B&B in a quiet, secluded cottage just off the B 2026. In the heart of the 6,500 acres of heathland, woodland and beautiful countryside of the Ashdown forest offering walking and wildlife in Winnie the Pooh country. Close to many Sussex tourist attractions, gardens, vegetarian pubs, castles and the sea. One double and one twin, both en suite with shower and wc, £36-42 per room including continental or hot breakfast with veggie sausages etc, vegan marg and muesli if you want it, soya milk, organic food whenever available. Single occupancy £25. Tea/coffee making and bedside clock/radio in rooms. TV lounge. Breakfast in rooms on request, the breakfast room or on a sunny, rose scented terrace in the garden. 5% discount for 4+ nights to VSUK, Vegan Society, Viva!, PeTA, Animal Aid, animal welfare organisations. Vegetarian and vegan evening meals by arrangement only and there is a good choice of local pubs serving all types of food. Pets welcome strictly by prior arrangement due to the resident friendly rescued animals. No smoking. People with mobility difficulties welcome, but please satisfy yourself by enquiries before booking.

Lewes

Seasons Vegetarian Café & Tea Room

119 High Street
Lewes
East Sussex BN7 2NS
Tel: 01273 473 968 Fax:
Tues-Sat 9.30-17.30

Family run vegetarian, organic with large vegan selection. Very environmentally friendly. Starters £2.50, Mains £3.95 brazil & cashew roast, beanburgers, spinach & potato pie. Salad bowl £2.50. Baked potatoes with fillings £2.60. Desserts 95p-£1.70 crumbles, apple cake, bakewell tart. Also cream teas with big selection of non caffeine alternatives.

Seaford

Salad Bowl

21 High Street
Seaford
East Sussex
Tel: 01323 890 605 Fax:
Open: Mon-Wed 9.30-14.00, Thu-Sat 9.30-16.00, closed Sun
Omnivorous café with veggie food and a veg hot pot for £2.15 which is very popular with local vegans. Also jacket potatoes.

Wadhurst

Wealden Wholefoods - Cafe and Takeaway

High Street
Wadhurst
East Sussex TN5 6AA
Tel: 01892 783 065 Fax:
Open: Mon-Sat 09.00-17.15 (Wed till 16.00, Sat 17.00)
Vegetarian wholefood café with take-away soup and sandwiches too. Savoury dishes 90p-£2.50 like Homity pie, quiche, homemade buckwheat and lentil slice, soups. Mixed salads £1-2. Homemade cakes, scones, flapjacks. Beer, tea 80p, coffee £1.05, soya milk.

HAMPSHIRE

Bishop's Waltham

Anchor Cottage

Bank Street
Bishop's Waltham
Hampshire SO32 1AN
Tel: 01489 894935 Fax:
1 double and 1 twin £32-£34, as singles £17-£19
Vegetarian bed and breakfast accommodation offered at modern cottage in attractive location close to historic village centre. 3 doors from White Swan pub should you build up a thirst. Easy walk to village centre for shopping or local nightlife. Between Winchester, Southampton and Portsmouth with nearby Meon Valley and those lovely Hampshire Downs. Bishops Waltham is off the B2177.

Brockenhurst

Broad Oak, formerly Lollard

Broadlands, Brockenhurst
Hampshire SO42 4PL
Tel: 01590 622208 Fax:
2 apartments, family sized, £18.50-£40
Unconventional b & b/self catering, own fridge and microwave, organic staple produce is supplied to use, when and how suits you. In magical spot in thriving New Forest town.

Havant

Country Kitchen

Havant Arts Centre
East Street, Havant
Hampshire PO9 1BS
Tel: 01705 486 505 Fax:
Mon-Sat 9.30-16.30
Vegetarian café in Arts centre where there is often an exhibition or other cultural activities. Soup of day £1.95, two bakes (1 always vegan) £3.25, pates, sandwiches, quiches, jacket spuds etc. Various desserts, coffee with free refills and news-

papers available. House wine £6.95.

Southampton

Ashlee Lodge

36 Atherley Road
Shirley, Southampton
Hampshire SO15 5DQ
Tel: 01703 222095 Fax:
1 single, 1 twin, 1 double, 1 family £16-£17
Vegetarian friendly b and b only. Plenty of pubs, restaurants or
even nearby chinese with veg selections.

Saffron Vegetarian Bistro

5 Bedford Place
Southampton
Hampshire SO15 2DB
Tel: 01703 369 666 Fax:
Mon-Tues 11.00-14.30, Wed-Sat 11.00-14.30 & 19.00-22.30
closed Sun.
All day breakfasts £2.20-£3, lunch menu includes soup of day
£2.40 nut loaf, curry, pasta & broccoli bake, chilli, homity pie,
all with salad or veg of day at £3.95. Jacket potatoes with various fillings £3.50-£3.90. Afternoon tea £2.95 and a selection of
cakes, scones, pastries, muffins and croissant. 3 course
evening meal for £12.95. Choice of 6 entrées: soup, Waldorf
salad, galeete, pakora, meze, avocado. 5 mains: Thai green
curry, veg crumble, mushroom strudel, stir fry or med veggies
in polenta. 5 desserts, 3 of which are vegan. Good value wine
list from £5.90 a bottle.

The Town House

59 Oxford Street, Southampton
Hampshire SO14 3DL
Tel: 01703 340 446 Fax:
Tues-Fri 12.00-14.00 & 19.00 till late, Sat 19.00 till late.
Closed Sun & Mon.

Vegetarian restaurant offering entrees from £1.55-£2.25 soups, hummous & dates, avocado, pate, bhajis etc. Main courses at £3.25 goulash, moussaka, crispy veg in sweet & sour or curry sauce, stuffed pancakes and jacket potatoes. Homemade desserts £2.50. 3 course dinner £12.95, similar entrees to lunch menu, mains like savoury kiev, peking roast, curried wellington, lasagne, spinach strudel served with fresh veg or salad. Dessert choice and a coffee with some home made fudge for 70p.

Southsea

The Amberley Guest House

37 Castle Road
Southsea
Hampshire PO5 3DE
Tel: 01705 850563 Fax:
1 single & 5 double from £25, includes dinner.
Veggie friendly guest house that's very handy for the Portsmouth ferry terminals. Also coastal and country walks. Price includes 3 course veg dinner that is based on the current residents' ideas.

Country Kitchen

59 Marmion Road
Southsea, Hampshire PO5 2AX
Tel: 01705 811 425 Fax:
Mon-Sat 9.30-17.00
Vegetarian wholefood restaurant, part of the Havant Arts Centre. Choice of soup £1.95, 3 bakes reg £3.25 and large portion £4.95, pates, jacket potatoes and selection of light snacks, apparently renowned for their quiches. Usual desserts and homemade cakes with free coffee refills and a selection of newspapers. Unlicensed but can bring your own.

ISLE OF WIGHT

Newport

God's Providence House

12 St Thomas's Square
Newport, Isle of Wight PO30 1SL
Tel: 01983 522 085 Fax:
Mon-Tues 9.00-17.30, Wed-Sat 9.00-17.00. Closed Sun
Large omnivorous restaurant with a few veggie dishes.

Whitwell

Divya-Krupa

Kenning Road
Whitwell
Isle of Wight PO38 2QT
Tel: 01983 731279 Fax:
1 single £15, 2 twin £15, 1 double en suite £20 March-October
Veg and vegan b&b that will also cope with almost any dietary
needs in a quiet and peaceful house with spacious gardens,
outdoor dining is an option. Usual veggie breakfasts and international cuisine dinner from £8.

KENT

Canterbury

Café des Amis

93 St Dunstan Street
Canterbury, Kent
Tel: 01227-464390 Fax:
Open every day 12-22.00
Busy omnivorous Mexican restaurant with lots of vegetarian
food which is a good place for us now that Canterbury's
Fungus Mungus veggie restaurant has closed, though it's a bit
too cheesey for vegans. Two sittings starting at 7-7.30pm and
9-9.30pm. Main courses from £7 up to £18 for a dish for two

people. Bookings for up to 12 people accepted in advance except Fri-Sat when the maximum is 6 of you. Near Westgate Towers.

The Tanner of Wingham Restaurant & B&B

44 High Street, Wingham
Canterbury, Kent CT3 1AB
Tel: 01227 720532 Fax: 01227 720532
1 single £20, 3 double, 2 en suite £39-£49. 1 family £49.
16th Century building on the village high street offering a veggie or vegan breakfast option. T/v, tea/coffee in rooms, bar (not in rooms). The restaurant always has a large vegetarian selection £15. 6 miles from Canterbury on A257.

Chatham

Food For Living Eats

116 High Street, Chatham
Kent ME4 4BY
Tel: 01634 409 291 Fax:
Open: Mon-Sat till 16.30, closed Sun
Vegetarian café with some vegan food. The veg bake is vegan but isn't on every day, just remember to ask them not to sprinkle cheese on it. All soups are vegan, as are the burgers and salad. Everything is cooked on the premises so they can tell you what's in it.

Folkestone

Holland & Barrett Restaurant

80 Sandgate Road, Folkestone
Kent CT20 2AA
Tel: 01303 243 646 Fax:
Mon-Sat 9.30-17.00 closed Sunday
Wholefood veggie café and take away in a Holland and Barrett shop. Selection of 6 salads 50p-£2.70, Bakes, quiches, baked spuds etc. £1-£2.10. And for that sweet tooth jellies, fruit tarts, cheesecakes £1.25-£1.55.

The India Restaurant

1 The Old High Street, Folkestone
Kent CT20 1RJ
Tel: 01303 259 155 Fax:
Tue-Sun 12.00-14.00 & 18.00-21.30 closed Mon
Indian restaurant with reasonable vegetarian choice.

Whitstable

El Loco

Oxford Street, Whitstable
Kent
Tel: 01227-771914 Fax:
Open: Tue-Sat 19-22.30, last food orders 22.00
New Mexican restaurant with plenty of vegetarian food, mostly
cheesey, on the site of the old veggie restaurant Beanies.
Vegans can have a vegetarian burrito £6 with lots of vegeta-
bles like aubergine plus beans, all cooked with sunflower oil -
just ask them to leave the cheese out.

SURREY

Camberley

Tekels Park Guest House

Tekels Park, Camberley
Surrey
Tel: 01276 23159 Fax: 01276 27014
Closed for 1 week over New Year.
Theosophical Society owned large vegetarian guest house in a
50 acre private estate, with a full compliment of wildlife. It is
ideal for a relaxing and revitalising break. 16 single rooms
£25.50-27.50; 1 double £45; 4 twin rooms £45; 1 twin en suite
£50; 1 family room £60. Tea/coffee, washbasins, TV in some
rooms, and also a TV lounge. Veggie and vegan breakfasts
available including muesli, soya milk & vegan marg. Manager
is vegan. Evening set meal £6.50 - vegetarian and vegan.
10% discount for Veggie and Vegan Society members. Good

facilities for group meetings.
Directions: leave M3 at Junction 3, follow A30 then A325 to large roundabout (over M3). Take Camberley turning.

Croydon

Hockney's

98 High Street, Croydon
Surrey CR0 1ND
Tel: 0181 688 2899 Fax: 0181 649 9375
Open: Tue-Thu, Sat 11-17.00, Fri 11-22.00. Closed Sun-Mon.
Vegetarian restaurant and café with dishes from around the world, half vegan. 10 main courses £6.95 include brazil and almond roast filled with mushroom and apricot stuffing with a tomato and dill sauce, served with hot vegetables; fruit curry with bananas, pineapple and peaches in a spicy curry sauce, with dhal and rice. Daytime menu has salads 70p-£3.45 including Waldorf and curried potato, falafel £3.25, jacket potato with filling £1.90, veggie burger £1.80, soup £1.80.
Desserts £1.95-2.95 such as vanilla Swedish Glace vegan ice-cream with warm maple syrup and chopped pecan nuts; banana and cashew vegan cake. Teas 80p, coffee 90p, they have soya milk. Bring your own booze, corkage £1.50.

Sunflower Café

67 South End
(opposite Blue Anchor pub)
Croydon, Surrey CR0 1BF
Tel: 0181-688 7433 Fax:
Completely vegetarian and vegan café. Set menu around £10 for 3 courses. Choice of four or five dishes per course. Bring your own booze, no corkage charge.

The Riverside Vegetaria

265 High St (near Leon House)
Croydon, Surrey CR0 1QH
Tel: 0181-688 7998 Fax:
Mon-Fri 12-15.00, 17.30-23.00, Sat 12-23.00, Sun 12-22.30
Opened following the success of the popular Riverside in
Kingston. Same name & menu, very different view. Big international cuisine menu with superb range of interesting vegan
options - you WILL be spoilt for choice. Starters £2.90-£3.90
interesting soups, spinach pate, Vadai (chick pea, green chilli,
spices, deep fried, with coconut sambal) yummy. Mains £4.95-
£5.95 masala dosai, paella, cous cous, nut roasts, lentil & ava-
cado kedgeree. Large portions - if you want dessert, be sure
you want a starter too! Speaking of desserts, there's a great
selection from £2.95. Selection of wines from £5.95 for half
bottle of frascati. Great place to convert carnivores.

Kingston

Riverside Vegetaria

64 High Street
Kingston-upon-Thames, Surrey
Tel: 0181-546 7992 Fax:
Mon-Fri 12-15.00, 17.30-23.00, Sat 12-23.00, Sun 12-22.30
Very popular, see Croydon branch listing for menu & prices.

Richmond

Rani

3 Hill Street
Richmond
Surrey TW9 1SX
Tel: 0181 332 2322 Fax:
Open: Tue-Thu 18.00-22.00, Fri & Sat 18.00-22.45, Sun
12.15-21.30
Indian vegetarian.

Richmond Harvest Restaurant

5 The Square, Richmond
Surrey TW9 1DT
Tel: 0181 940 1138 Fax:
Mon-Sat 11.30-23.00, Sun 12.30-20.00
International wholefood vegetarian restaurant. Mostly vegan starters £3.50-£4.50 pinto hummous, aubergine with tahini, tamari mushrooms. Mains such as aubergine Kashmir, courgette cashew casserole, cauliflower bake, leek lasagne, jacket spuds and various salads. Six desserts including fruit crumble, chocolate banana pudding, banoffi pie. Good wine list from £7.50.

Tide Tables

2 The Archways, Richmond Bridge
Richmond, Surrey TW9 1TH
Tel: 0181-948 8285 Fax:
Open: Summer every day 9-21.00. Winter weekdays 11-19.00,
weekends 11-19.00
New vegetarian café with a riverside terrace in a very beautiful spot on the Thames. Menu varies with quiche, lasagne, mousakka, bakes, hot pots, savoury rolls etc. Also large range of sandwiches, salads, handmade cakes, teas, espresso coffee and they have soya milk. Bring your own booze, no corkage charge.

WEST SUSSEX

Arundel

Country Life

The Old Candle Factory, 1 Terrant Square
Terrant Street, Arundel
West Sussex
Tel: 01903 883 456 Fax:
Every day except Thurs 10.30-17.00 also Fri/Sat 19.00-22.00
Around half the menu is vegetarian, gratins, hot-pots, spaghetti

provencale etc.

Chichester

Cafe Paradiso

Longlime Ltd
9 Priory Lanes, Northgate
Chichester, West Sussex PO19 1AR
Tel: 01243 532 967 Fax:
Mon-Sat 9.00-17.00 closed Sunday.
Vegetarian café.

St Martins Tearooms

3 St Martins St
Chichester, West Sussex
Tel: 01243 786715 Fax:
Mon-Sat 9.00-18.00 closed Sunday.
Organic wholefood tearoom in the attractive Chichester town centre, close to the cross. They also serve cooked lunches, tomato & basil soup, courgette bake etc. from a choice of 4 dishes. All savoury dishes, soups and cakes are made on the premises and a list of their ingredients are available at the counter. Health food that is without unnecessary saturated fats and sugars. No microwave, no aluminium pans, they don't even have a tin opener! All veggie apart from the odd unlucky fish.

Clinchs Salad House

14 Southgate
Chichester, West Sussex PO19 1ES
Tel: 01243 788 822 Fax:
Mon-Fri 8.00-17.30 Sat 7.30-17.30 Sun closed
Primarily vegetarian wholefood café, offering lots of salads £1.80-£2.50, sandwiches, mains £2.95 nut roast, curry, bakes, gratin, baked spuds etc.

Horsham

East Mews Revival Cafe

5a Park Place
(next to Pirie's Place)
Horsham, West Sussex RH12 1DF
Tel: 01403-271 125 Fax:
Completely vegetarian and vegan café. Set menu around £10 for 3 courses with a choice of 4 or 5 dishes per course. Bring your own booze with no corkage charge.

Plaistow

Clements Vegetarian Restaurant

Rickmans Lane
Plaistow (near Billingshurst)
West Sussex RH14 0NT
Tel: 01403-871 246 Fax:
Open: Tue-Sat 19-23.00 (last orders 21.30)
Vegetarian and vegan restaurant. One of the most up-market veggie places in the UK, around £20 for three courses and drinks. At least two vegan dishes per course. Typical vegan dishes to start are falafels with red pepper and green chilli sauce; avocado, grapefruit and kiwi salad. Main courses might be cashew and vegetable koftas served with vegetable tikka masala and brown and wild rice; leek, mushroom and capsicum Wellington. Finish with a chocolate and rum cheesecake (tofu) or blackcurrant and apple crumble pie. Will open lunchtimes for large groups.
Directions: On the main road through the village of Plaistow. Ring them if you want a copy of the current menu and a map, as people travel from far and wide to this unique restaurant.

Worthing

Seasons Restaurant

15 Crescent Road
Worthing, West Sussex BN11 1RL
Tel: 01903 236 011 Fax:
Open: Mon-Fri 9-15.00, Sat 9-16.00
Vegetarian café and restaurant with food from various cuisines.

Entrées £1 like soups with granary bread. 3 vegan and 3 veggie salads 70p-£3.50 such as carrot and orange, beansprouts, watercress and peppers, coleslaw, curried veg, tomato and garlic, pasta etc. 2 vegan and 2 veggie main courses which change daily, £3.50, could be Brazil nut loaf, leek and mushroom satay, curry pizza, pasta dishes, Brazil shepherd's pie, bean dishes, casseroles etc. Plus jacket potatoes, quiches, fresh scones and homemade cakes. 2 veggie and 2 vegan desserts £1.50 like crumbles, fruit salad, trifle, fruit pies, fruit fools and many traditional puddings. Well this is the British seaside. Coffee 70p, soya milk. No booze.

The Nuthouse Vegetarian Restaurant

29 Marine Parade
Worthing, West Sussex BN11 3PT
Tel: 01903 239 009 Fax:
Mon-Sat 12.00-15.00 & 18.00-21.30 Sunday 12.00-15.00
Mainly vegan.

LONDON

ACCOMMODATION

Barrow House

45 Barrow Road
Streatham Common, London SW16 5PE
Tel: 0181 6771925 Fax:
Streatham Common British Rail and close to the A23
Vegetarian and vegan bed and breakfast. Luxurious accommodation is offered just 15 minutes by rail from Victoria Station in this Victorian family house situated in a quiet location. Two doubles and two singles £45, or £30 as a single. Breakfast features fruit salad, cereal and toast, and there are a few vegetarian restaurants in Streatham.

Dora Rothner Bed and Breakfast

23 The Ridgeway
Finchley, London N3 2PG
Tel: 0181 346 0246 Fax:
Private bed and breakfast where they're used to doing vegetarian or vegan breakfasts. 2 doubles and 1 single for £15 per person. Handy for Finchley Road tube (Northern line), the North Circular and M1.

Hampstead Village Guesthouse

2 Kemplay Road
Hampstead, London NW3 1SY
Tel: 0171-435 8679 Fax: 0171-794 0254
vguesthouse@gn.apc.org
5 rooms from £35-£90 with all amenities in rooms.
Veggie friendly. Victorian house in lively Hampstead Village, fun area with art cinema, loads of restaurants, coffee shops and pubs. A must see for visitors.

Mount View

31 Mount View Road, London N4 4SS
Tel: 0181 340 9222 Fax: 0181 342 8494
3 doubles, 1 en suite £40-£50

Veggie friendly, all rooms with t/v and tea/coffee, no evening meal but not a problem in "villagy" Crouch End, also a bit cheaper than the West End prices. Within walking distance of Finsbury Park tube and rail station, luggage can be collected when you arrive there.

Parkland Walk Guesthouse

12 Hornsey Rise Gardens
London N19 3PR
Tel: 0171 263 3228 Fax: 0171 831 9489
2 double, 2 single £28-£65 most en suite.

Veggie friendly, with vegan options in award winning guest house, tea/coffee, t/v and radio in rooms. 5 minutes from Alexandra Palace with those great views over London, Highgate cemetery and village are both nearby. From North Circular/M1 follow signs for A1 Archway direction till North Hill leading to Highgate Village, then Hornsey Lane over the viaduct with Hornsey Rise Gardens on your right. Archway underground or Hornsey Rise railway.

Regents Park Guesthouse

Regents Park Road, London NW1 8XP
Tel: 0171 722 7139 Fax: 0171 586 3004

Prior booking essential for 2 double/twin rooms one with own bathroom other with own shower, becomes self contained apartment with living room when both rooms taken. £50-60 per night, single £35-40 with inclusive breakfast. Ideal central London location 2 min walk to underground, free street parking, Primrose Hill and Regents Park nearby.

Sylvia Wills

95 Queens Road, East Sheen, London SW14 8PH
Tel: 0181-878 2917 Fax:
Veggie and vegan B&B. One small single room overlooking
the garden £22.50 with TV. Strictly non-smoking female only.
Off Upper Richmond Road (South Circular), close to Barnes
Cemetary and hospital and Richmond Park.   Taste of Raj
restaurant on corner of Queens Road. 10% discount for
Vegan and Veg Soc, Viva!, PETA, Animal Aid.

Temple Lodge

51 Queen Caroline Street, Hammersmith, London W6 9QL
Tel: 0181-748 8388 Fax:
Large Georgian house run by The Christian Community offering bed and breakfast accommodation. 2 singles £25, 3+
nights £22, £140 week. 4 twins £35, £190 week, which can be
let as singles at the single rate. Washbasins in rooms. No TV.
Continental vegetarian breakfast but vegans must request
ahead. Classy vegetarian restaurant The Gate at same
address. Close to the Thames and Olympia or Earls Court
Exhibition Centres. Underground connection to the West End.

The Lanesborough

Hyde Park Corner, London SW1X 7TA
Tel: 0171-259 5599 Fax: 0171-259 5606
For reservations in USA call toll free 1 800 999 1828
fax 1 800 937 8278   www.rosewood-hotels.com
Luxury hotel popular with veggie rock and movie stars.
Singles from £225, doubles from £300 up to the royal suite for
£3500. Services include 24 hour butler, fitness studio, health
club membership, video and CD in your room with a free
library, all the sybaritic delights anyone could wish for. The in-
house restaurant The Conservatory features the new *Menu
Potager*, a seven-course gourmet vegetarian dinner, prepared
by top chef Paul Gayler or one of his brigade of 40 chefs.
Express lunch £11 which includes a main course, breads and
glass of wine. 2 or 3 course lunch £19.50 or £23.50. Dinner -
bring your credit card - from £28.50.

CENTRAL LONDON

OUTER LONDON

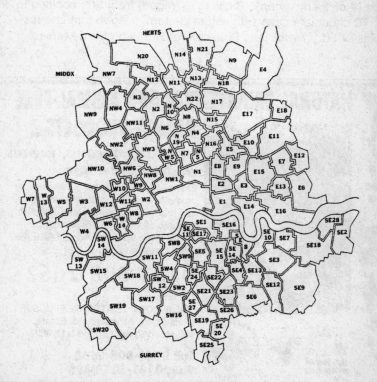

WEST END RESTAURANTS

Beatroot

92 Berwick Street
Soho, London W1
Tel: 0171-437 8591
Open: Mon-Sat 9.00-19.00

London's fantastic brand new swish vegetarian and 80% vegan café at the pedestrianised south end of Berwick Street by the fruit and veg market. 10 hot dishes, 8 of them vegan, for £2.50, £3.50 or £4.50 including your choice of any of the 6 salads (4 of them vegan). 8 cakes (6 vegan) from 50p cookies to £1.70 chocolate cake with vegan custard. Vegan tofu cheesecake £1.50. (Herb) teas 90p, coffee £1. Two outside tables.

Country Life

3-4 Warwick Street, London W1
Tel: 0171-434 2922. Tube: Piccadilly Circus
Open: Sun -Fri 11.30-15.00, 17.00-22.00. Closed Fri eve, Sat.
London's central vegan restaurant is reopening May 1998
close to Piccadilly. Brilliant buffet all-you-can-eat lunch of
mixed salads and hot dishes which you pay for according to
weight, roughly £5-6 a plate. Awesome desserts. Afternoon tea
15-17.30. Evenings they've gone up-market à la carte, last
orders 21.00. Superb wholefood shop open Mon-Wed 9-
18.00, Thu till 19.30, Fri till 15.00 winter or 18.00 summer, Sun
11.30-16.00. Also cookery classes, meeting room. Alex's all-
time fave restaurant to be visited at every opportunity.

Cranks Marshall Street

8 Marshall Street, Soho, London W1
Tel: 0171-437 9431
Open: Mon-Sat 08.00-20.00, closed Sun.
Huge vegetarian health food café with counter service.
Average £5 with two salads. Plenty for vegans including at
least one cake.

Raw Deal Vegetarian Restaurant

65 York Street, Marylebone
London W1H 1PQ
Tel: 0171-262 4841 Fax: 0171 258 1131
Open: Mon-Fri 08.00-22.00. Closed Sat-Sun.
Vegetarian restaurant near Baker Street. Menu changes daily
with a soup and two hot dishes, one always vegan. Also jacket
potatoes with fillings, 12 salads 85p-£2.50 or platters £3.50-
5.50. Main courses £5.50-6.50 such as nutty aubergine; sweet
corn fritters with mixed veg; aduki bean lasagne; mushroom
roll. All homemade desserts £1.75-2.50 include bread and
butter pudding, vegan apricot crumble. Beer £2.50. House
wine £7.50 bottle, £1.75 glass. Tea 60p, coffee 90p, soya milk.

Woodlands Restaurant

77 Marylebone Lane
(off Marylebone High St)
London W1M 4GA
Tel: 0171-486 3862
Open: 7 days for lunch and dinner

Vegetarian Indian restaurant. Big menu with plenty of savouries for vegans. Starters like samosa and bhel poori £1.70-2.25. Dosas £2.50-3.50, uthappam lentil pizza £2.75 plus 30p per extra topping. Veg korma curry with cashews and rice £3.95. Thalis £6.25 or £7.25. Steamed, lemon, coconut, bakala or pillau rice £1.50-2.75. Party bookings welcome.

Cranks St Christopher's Place

23 Barrett Street
London W1M 5HP
Tel: 0171-495 1340
Open: Mon-Fri 8.00-19.30 (Thu 20.30), Sat 9.00-19.00, closed
Sun
Vegetarian health food with cracking wholefood dishes for veggies and vegans. Average £5-6. Almost opposite Bond Street tube station, down an alleyway past Dillons bookshop that leads to a pedestrian area.

Mandeer Restaurant

21 Hanway Place
off Tottenham Court Rd
London W1P 9DG
Tel: 0171-323 0660 Fax:
Open: Mon-Sat 12-15.00, 17.30-22.00. Closed Sun.
London's oldest vegetarian restaurant, serving top quality Indian Ayurvedic gourmet cuisine since 1961. Big lunchtime buffet lunch £2.90-5.00 will get you a Veganosaurus Rex sized platter of bhajia, samosa, brown rice, veg, chickpeas and dhal, and you can chat to other veggiesaurs at the long table. In the evening they go upmarket a la carte. Starters like dal vada, pani puri, kachori, dosa or samosa £2.25-4.95. Punjabi dishes £3.75-4.95 like Bombay alu, tofu curry, tarka dal £3.75-5.50. Gujarati dishes include vegetable curry, beans of the day or vadi and onion. Basic vegan thali £8 ranging up to a Mandeer Deluxe £12.50 of pilau rice, bread, panir matar, Bomay alu, veg curry, beans, samosa, vada, papadom and chutney, dessert. Heaps of dairy based desserts plus 4 fruity ones for vegans, £2.50. Coffee or tea £1. Fully licensed. Threatened with closure by a developer from Spring 98 so phone first and watch out for a new location.

Cranks Tottenham Street

9-11 Tottenham Street
near Goodge St underground
London W1P 9PB
Tel: 0171-631 3912
Open: Mon-Fri 8.00-19.00, Sat 9-19.30, closed Sun
Vegetarian health food restaurant and shop. Fill up for £5. In the afternoon you can sit quietly in the back with a herb tea and the papers.

Wagamama

10A Lexington Street
London W1R 3HS
Tel: 0171-292 0990 Fax: 0171-734 1815
Open: Mon-Sat 12-23.00, Sun 12.30-22.00.
Fast food Japanese noodle bar with nine veggie and vegan dishes. Very busy, totally authentic, heaps of fun. Allow about £10. See WC1 branch for menu.

Nuthouse Vegetarian Restaurant

26 Kingly Street, London W1R 5LB
Tel: 0171-437 9471
Open: Mon-Sat 10.30-19.30. Closed Sun.

Vegetarian café round the back of Liberty and Hamleys mega toy store, close to Oxford Circus. Great value munchies for West End shoppers to eat in (or take out) like baked potato £1.65 (£1.50), £3 (£2.50) with beans. Nut rissoles with tomato and onion sauce £1.75 (£1.55). Small salad £2.50 (2.25), large £3.50 (3.25). Two main courses daily £3.25 like mousakka, vegetable pancake, mixed beans casserole, stir fry. Cakes and beverages. What you see is what you pay: none of the usual cover or service or VAT "extras" and they won't take tips.

Govinda's Vegetarian Restaurant

9/10 Soho Street, Soho, London W1V 5DA
Tel: 0171-437 3662 Fax: 0171-437 4928
Open: Mon-Sat 12-20.00, closed Sun

Very friendly wholefood vegan and lacto-vegetarian Indian restaurant and café with some Chinese and fast food run by those nice Hare Krsna people, next door to their temple, smack in the middle of London near the Tottenham Court Road end of Oxford Street. 2 vegan and 4 veggie starters such as pakoras or dahl with bread £1.50. 7 vegan and 9 veggie choices to make your large £3.75 or regular £2 mixed salad. 3 vegan and 10 veggie main course dishes, but the best value of all is the 7 dish all-you-can-eat buffet £4.99. You can go back for more, though Godzilla would have trouble finishing even the first round. As well as Indian food they have lasagne, quiche, pizza, veggie-burgers and baked potatoes for £1.50-3.00. Up to 10 veggie but only 1 vegan dessert, usually a very yummy cake. But hey, they do have soya milk, soya milkshakes and no eggs. Lots of juices and waters 75p-£1.20. (Decaf) tea or coffee or herb tea 80p. Non smoking. Surplus grub is given to London's homeless after hours.

Mildreds

58 Greek Street, Soho, London W1V 5LR
Tel: 0171-494 1634 Fax: 0171-494 1634
Open: Mon-Sat 12-23.00, Sun 12.30-18.30
Almost completely vegetarian café-restaurant and take-away in the heart of vibrant restaurant land serving all kinds of food on a menu that changes daily. Starters £2.30-3.50 like dahl with coconut cakes or artichoke soup. Main courses £4.50-5.80 are mostly vegan such as warm Catalan butter bean salad with caramelized fennel and leeks plus olive bread; lentil, courgette and pumpkin seed burger with aubergine, apricot relish and garlic mayonnaise served with salad and New York fries; stir fried veg in sesame oil with garlic and ginger on brown rice. Falafel £4.70 or take-away £2.80. Salads £2.20-5.00. At least one of the 8 more-ish desserts is vegan such as rich chocolate pudding £2.95, extra soya cream 60p. Organic house wine £8.20 bottle, £2.30 glass. Teas and coffees 80p-£1.50. They have soya milk.

Veeraswamy's

99-101 Regent Street, London W1R 7HB
Tel: 0171-734 1401
Open every day 12-14.30, 17.30-23.30 (Sun -22.00)
London's oldest omnivorous Indian restaurant and possibly its most opulent, with North and South Indian dishes on its separate vegetarian menu. Average meal £25.

Zazoom

3 New Burlington Street, (off Regent Street)
London W1X 1FD
Tel: 0171-287 1991
Open: they never close
If there are 30 veggie restaurants in central London, why are we listing this omnivorous one? Easy - this one is open all night 7 days a week and has 28 veggie dishes on the menu though lean pickings for vegans. It's FUN and funky with live music, DJ's and MTV screens - a place more unlike a vegetarian restaurant is hard to imagine! And it's bang in the middle of

the west end close to Oxford Street tube, next to Samantha's Discotheque. 6 veggie starters £1.50-2.45 like Cajun mushrooms, homous in pitta or tabbooleh. Falafel £3.95. Salads and side dishes £1.50-2.50. Baked potato £1.55, or with beans £2.05. Veggie burger £4.25. Veg stir fry with tortilla £5.50. 10 non vegan desserts from £1.95. Coffee 90p. Bottled beers £2.10. Happy hours from 5-8pm with all drinks and cocktails half price.

Prince Charles Cinema

Leicester Place, north side of Leicester Square
London W1
Tel: 0171-494 4087. www.digitalmedia.demon.co.uk
Bargain alert!! Not a restaurant, not a café, but the cheapest cinema in London charging £1.75 in the daytime, or £2.25 evenings and weekends. The films are almost new including blockbusters, with five different ones on every day, for a third of the price of other West End cinemas. There are even free postcards in the basement, plus a bar serving all drinks for £2. This will leave you with heaps more dough for the 30 veggie restaurants and cafés in the West End. If you're a student or on a budget we recommend preceding or following your cinema outing with a visit to the all-you-can-scoff £4.99 buffet at Govinda's on the north side of Soho Square. Or buy your ticket and grab a falafel for £2 at a café on the NE corner of Leicester Square, about 100m from the cinema. Call above number for today's programme or 0171-4378181 for the whole week.

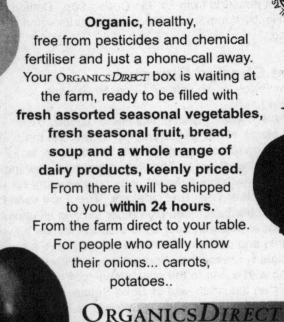

BLOOMSBURY WC1

Chambali

146 Southampton Row
Bloomsbury, London WC1
Tel: 0171-837 3925 Fax:
Open: 12-24.00 every day
Omnivous North Indian restaurant open really late, with heaps of vegetarian food such as thali for around £12 or vegetable biryani with curry sauce £9.

Wagamama

4 Streatham Street, off Bloomsbury St,
Bloomsbury, London WC1A 1JB
Tel: 0171-323 9223 Fax: 0171-323 9224
Open: Mon-Sat 12-23.00, Sun 12.30-22.00.
Fast food Japanese noodle bar with nine veggie and vegan dishes. Order your drinks from the mobile drinks waiter while you queue for about 20 minutes. Refectory atmosphere with long trestle tables and very noisy. Not recommended for a first date, but brill for a cram of students or a giggle of Spices out on the town for a laff. Starters £2.80-3.40 like yasai gyoza, agedashi tofu or edamame. Raw salad £2.50. Mains £4.50-5.50 such as yasai yaki soba (noodles), yasai chilli men, moyashi soba, yasai katsu curry, yasai cha han. All dishes served together.

Greenhouse

Drill Hall, 16 Chenies Street
Bloomsbury, London WC1E 7EX
Tel: 0171-637 8038 Fax:
Open: Mon-Fri 12-22.30, Sat 12-20.00, Sun 12-17.00
Vegetarian basement restaurant with global food and a friendly atmosphere. Good sized portions, lots of homemade, non pious, tasty food. Vegan soup £2, main meal £4 such as gado gado and rice, roast potato and aubergine stew (both vegan),

moussaka, lasagne, curries, bakes, burgers. Desserts and cakes from 60p and there's always something vegan.

World of Difference
14 Woburn Walk
Bloomsbury, London WC1H 0JL
Tel: 0171-387 2363 Fax:
Open: Mon-Sat 11-18.00
The green shop in the heart of London, close to Euston station. Low energy lightbulbs, battery chargers, insulation, recycled paper, refillable toner cartridges, washable nappies and Weleda baby lotions, toiletries, crafts, Fair Trade goods. Non leather shoes, belts, clothes and bags. Also animal rights and vegetarian books and green magazines. Woburn walk is full of half-timbered buildings and popular with film-makers, so any tourists reading this be sure to bring your cameras.

COVENT GARDEN WC2

Cranks Covent Garden
The Piazza, Covent Garden
London WC2
Tel: 0171-379 6508 Fax:
Open: Mon-Sat 9-20.00 or later, Sun 11-19.00
Vegetarian health food café on two levels with a terrace, offering Mediterranean syle food for about £5, plus heaps of cakes. Always something for vegans.

Cranks Express
8 Adelaide Street, London WC2
Tel: 0171-836 0660 Fax:
Open: Mon-Sat 08.00-20.00, Sun 12-17.00
Vegetarian fast health food café and take-away close to Charing Cross station. Sandwiches, stir-fry, pizza, quiche, hot

dish of the day, soups, salads, juices and cakes. There's always something vegan. Small eating area.

Eden Rock Café

22 Cranbourne Street, (by Leicester Square)
London WC2
Tel: 0171-379 7737 Fax:
Open: 7 days 08.00-03.00
Omnivorous Lebanese café open till 3 in the morning, close to the Hippodrome, Stringfellows, theatres and cinemas, and the Trafalgar Square night buses. Midnight munchies for revellers include falafel £3.75 (take-away £3.40), aubergine salad £2.95, mixed veg £2.95, tabouleh £2.40, veg soup £2.40. Large mixed vegetarian deli £5.95 with tabouleh, aubergine, rice, humous and salads. Chips £1 take-away. Lavazza coffee £1.50. Kaliber £1.50.

Jubilee Hall Sports Centre

30 The Piazza, Covent Garden
London WC2E
Tel: 0171-836 4007 Fax:
Open: Mon-Fri 07.00-22.00. Sat-Sun 10-17.00.
Mostly veggie café serving wholefoods, Chinese and English grub from where you can ogle the "Westenders" pumping iron. 5 vegan and 10 veggie salad portions 50p-£1 like Waldorf, potato, spinach, tomato, five bean. 1 vegan and 9 veggie savouries such as veg risotto, hotpot, stuffed peppers, baked avocado with sun ripe tomatoes. Teas or coffee 65p. No soya milk.

Cranks Leicester Square

17 Great Newport Street, London WC2H 7JE
Tel: 0171-836 5226 Fax:
Open: Mon-Fri 08.00-21.00, Sat 10-21.00, Sun 12-21.00
Vegetarian health food café where you can fill up for a fiver or

just have a coffee. Busy early evening with the post-work pre-cinema crowd, otherwise the perfect place to write a postcard while waiting for a friend. Just east of Leicester Square.

First Out Coffee Shop

52 St Giles High St, St Lukes
London WC2H 8LH
Tel: 0171-240 8042 Fax:
Open: Mon-Sat 11-23.00, Sun 11-20.30
Gay and lesbian vegetarian and fish café with plenty of vegan food at low prices. London Vegetarian and Vegan Gay and Bisexual Men's group meets here on the last Sunday of every month, friends and women welcome, phone 0181-690 4792 for details. Handy for the nearby gay nightclubs.

Carrie Awaze Designer Sandwiches

27 Endell Street, Covent Garden
London WC2H 9BA
Tel: 0171-836 0815 Fax:
Open: Mon-Fri 9.30-20.00, Sat 12-19.30, Sun 12-17.00.
Omnivorous Indian and international vegetarian and vegan take-away. Soup £2.25 or take out £1.25. 6 vegan and 21 veggie sandwiches £1.95-2.25 take-away or £2.35-2.70 eat in, such as "Brown Bomber" onion bhajia with houmous and salad. 4 vegan and 3 veggie fillings with jacket spud and salad £4.50-6.25 such as "Arne Street" dhal and onion bhajia. Vegetarian thali or curry and rice £4.95. Desserts of which fresh fruit salad is vegan. Beer £2.25 with food, wine £9.50 bottle or £2.25 glass. Herb tea or coffee £1.25 and they have soya milk. S.E. England winner of the Guardian's sensational sandwich competition.

Neal's Yard Bakery Co-op

6 Neal's Yard, Covent Garden
London WC2H 9DP
Tel: 0171-836 5199 Fax:
Open: Mon-Sat 10.30-17.00
One of three vegetarian cafés in Neal's Yard, this one special-
ising in organic bread and rolls. It's a bakery and tearoom with
a good range of vege-favourites for around £4. Grab an
organic loaf on the way out and buy some fillings at Neal's
Yard Wholefoods nearby.

Neal's Yard Salad Bar

2 Neal's Yard, Covent Garden
London WC2H 9DP
Tel: 0171-836 3233 Fax:
Open: Every day 11-21.00
Vegan owned vegetarian wholefood café with food prepared in
the open kitchen before your very eyes, with a Brazilian and
Oriental twist. Point to the food you want at the counter then
chill out in the sun at an outside table. Different foods daily
with three salads £2.70-3.20, dairy and wheat free vegetable
soup £1, main courses £3.60-4.00 such as Lebanes ekibe with
onion, fresh coriander and peppers; roasted aubergine stuffed
with tomato, onion and coriander; broccoli red pepper quiche.
Desserts £2.50-3.00 such as Brazilian banana cinnamon cake,
sweet corn pudding, tropical fruit trifle. Tea £1.20, coffee £1.50,
soya milkshakes too.

Neal's Yard World Food Café

First Floor, 14 Neal's Yard
Covent Garden, London WC2H 9DP
Tel: 0171-379 0298 Fax:
Open: Mon-Sat 12-17.00 (20.00 Wed & Thu)
Upstairs international wholefood vegetarian restaurant in the
heart of veggieland. Light meals £4.95-5.25 such as Indian

spicy veg masala with steamed brown rice; falafel with salad and houmous. Small mixed salad £4. Soup of the day £3.85. Big meals £6.95 could be thali with steamed brown rice; Turkish meze of aubergine and cabbage cooked with parsley, mint and tomatoes served with tabouleh salad, olives, mashed carrot, houmous and roasted pitta bread; West African or Mexican dishes; Large mixed plate of all the day's salads with guacamole, carrot, houmous, olives and pitta. Cakes, puddings, teas, coffes, juices. Minimum charge £4.85 at lunchtime and Saturdays.

Bunjies Coffee House

27 Litchfield Street, Covent Garden
London WC2H 9NJ
Tel: 0171-240 1796 Fax:
Open: Mon-Sat 12-23.00, closed Sun
Vegetarian basement bar-café with various live performers in the cellar end in the evening such as folk and comedy, which will cost you about £3. Filling basic grub includes veg mousaka or lasagne for around £4. Vegans can have ratatouille or curry with brown rice. A brilliant place to fill up after a movie. Just north of Leicester Square, on the east side of Charing Cross Road.

Food For Thought

31 Neal Street, Covent Garden
London WC2H 9PR
Tel: 0171-836 0239 Fax:
Open: Mon-Sat 9.30-20.30, Sun 12-16.00
Fabulous veggie take-away and basement café-restaurant offering superb value and ultra-fresh food from around the world. Menu changes daily so here are some examples: vegan Tuscan tomato and bread soup finished with olive oil and fresh basil £2.20; choice of 4 salads £1.50-4.50 such as potato and tofu mayonnaise. 4 main courses £2-3.40, at least one of them vegan, such as hot pot, stroganoff, cous cous royale, stir-fried veg. Or really tuck in to a seasonal plate of

main course plus salads £5.50. Several desserts £2.20-2.50
such as vegan plum and apple crumble. Cakes from 80p, half
of them vegan. Drinks 60p-£1 and they have soya milk. Alex
feasts here at every opportunity and so will you.

CAMDEN & EUSTON NW1

Euston

Health Food Centre
11 Warren Street, London NW1
Tel: 0171-387 9289 Fax:
Open: Mon-Fri 08.00-16.30 or later
Vegetarian health food shop and take-away with a huge variety
of hot and cold pastries, savouries, pies, snacks, salads, cakes
and the biggest range of sandwiches and rolls, many great for
vegans. Later in the afternoon they knock the remaining sandwiches down to £2 for two. Next to Warren Street tube station.

Diwana Bhelpoori House
121-123 Drummond Street
Euston, London NW1 2HL
Tel: 0171-380 0730. Open: Every day 12.00-23.45
Vegetarian South Indian restaurant. Busy all you can eat buffet
at lunchtime for £5 with a carafe of water on the table, a la
carte evening. Vegans can have lots of starters like bhajias,
but the main courses like dosas often contain dairy products.
Save money by bringing your own wine from the offie next
door for a minimal corkage chage.

Ravi Shankar
133-135 Drummond Street
Euston, London NW1 2HL
Tel: 0171-388 6458 Fax:
Open every day 12-23.00 (last order 22.30)

Great value vegetarian South Indian restaurant in the street of veggie Indians close to Euston station. There's always plenty for vegans including cashew nut pilau, pancakes and loads of veg.

Chutneys

124 Drummond Street
Euston, London NW1 2PA
Tel: 0171-387 6077 Fax:
Open: Every day 12.00-14.45, 18.00-23.30
Vegetarian South Indian restaurant. Really good vegan thali for £5.95 that's better than the £8-9 ones you'll find elsewhere. Buffet lunch for about a fiver. Licensed and quite swish with lots of people having quiet dinners and the odd party.

St Marylebone Café

St Marylebone Church Crypt
17 Marylebone Road, Marylebone
London NW1 5LT
Tel: 0171-935 6374 Fax:
Open: Mon-Fri 8.30-15.00
Vegetarian basement café with soups, casseroles, pasta and rice dishes, sandwiches, puddings, and always one vegan option. Free corkage. May close early if all the food goes. Disabled access and toilet.

Camden

The Raj

19 Camden High Street
Camden Town, London NW1 7JE
Tel: 0171-388 6663 Fax:
Open: Mon-Fri 12-15.00, 19-23.30. Sat-Sun 12-23.30.
Bargain alert!! Vegetarian South Indian restaurant with a 28 dish all-you-can-eat buffet every day. It costs a ludicrously reasonable £3.50 for lunch, £3.75 in the evening, £3.75 all day at weekends. The buffet features 28 vegetarian dishes and includes salads and puddings. There's a great value a la carte menu too.

Cafe Seventy Nine

79 Regents Park Road
London NW1 8UY
Tel: 0171-586 8012 Fax:
Open every day 8.30-18.30
Vegetarian café and take-away with a small number of seats outside in one of London's most picturesque streets on the edge of Primrose Hill park, catering for the lunchtime and weekend trade predominantly. Usual soups, bakes and dish of the day, salads, veggie burgers, toasted sandwiches and filled baguettes. A range of cakes and desserts including a vegan apple crumble. Milk shakes can be made with soya milk.

SLOANE ZONE SW1, 3 & 6

The Wren at St James's

35 Jermyn Street, St James, London SW1
Tel: 0171-437 9419 Fax:
Open: Mon-Sat 08.00-19.00, Sun 09.00-16.00
Vegetarian café next to the church on Piccadilly, with entrances on both sides of the block. Several main courses for around £4, soups, sarnies and carrot cake. Not a lot for vegans though usually something. They have outside tables and there's a garden in the churchyard.

Woodlands Vegetarian Restaurant

37 Panton St, (off Haymarket)
London SW1Y 4EA
Tel: 0171-839 7258 Fax:
Open: 7 days for lunch and dinner
Vegetarian Indian restaurant off the south-west corner of Leicester Square. Big menu with plenty of savouries for vegans. Starters like samosa and bhel poori £170-2.25. Lots of dosas £2.50-3.50, a South Indian crepe made from a batter of soaked and finely ground lentils and rice, fermented overnight

and served with a lentil soup and coconut chutney. Uthappam is a lentil pizza for £2.75 plus 30p per extra topping. Veg korma curry with cashews and rice £3.95. Thalis £6.25 or £7.25. Steamed, lemon, coconut, bakala or pillau rice £1.50-2.75.

Veg of Knightsbridge

8 Egerton Garden Mews
Knightsbridge, London SW3 2EH
Tel: 0171-584 7007 Fax:
Open: Every day 18.00-23.15, also lunch Tue-Fri 12-14.00.
Chinese vegan restaurant with reasonable prices close to Harrods. 18 entrées £3.00-6.50, 2 salads £2.50-3.50, 40 main courses £4.50-8.50. Desserts £3. Set meal £12. With offerings such as Veg-Oysters and Sweet & Sour Veg-Chicken, imitation meats are the speciality here in many different forms. Genuine ingredients are used: real seaweed (not cabbage) and naturally brewed soy sauce. The Vegetarian Dim Sum comes with a surprising and refreshing hot chili dip. Deep-fried Veg Oysters comprise aubergines and seaweed in batter. Tofu and Spinach Soup is a light classical Chinese variety. Seasonal vegetables are perfect: stir fried broccoli, pak soy and mange tout in a light sauce. Crispy Vegetarian Duck (deep-fried tofu skin) is rich, yet light as the wafer-thin pancakes it's wrapped in. Veg Beef in Black Bean Sauce is made from a traditional Chinese wheat gluten dish; a strong, meat-like taste. Veg uses staple Oriental ingredients to provide satisfying dishes which are often lacking in more western-style vegetarian diets. It is the classical styles of cooking particular to Chinese cuisine, along with subtle spices, that make the food here so wholesome and appetizing. Veg is not your typical veggie joint - here you have the perfect vegetarian menu without the, let's face it, queuing for the buffet, heavy whole-wheat pastry scenario. (Review by Tracey Scollin)

Mamta

692 Fulham Road, Fulham, London SW6
Tel: 0171-736 5914 Fax:
Open for lunch Wed-Sat 12.30-14.30, dinner every day 18.00-22.30
Indian vegetarian restaurant. 12 starters £2.10-4.15 from samosas to masala dhosa. Veg and curried veg £3.45-4.15 including tofu curry. Main course chef's specials £5.15-5.95 like aubergine and potatoes, fresh spinach, Bombay alu. 8 kinds of rice including brown with whole wheat and nuts and raisins or mushrooms and onions or tahini £2-2.95. Vegetable biriyani and rice £5.95. Dals £1.80-2.95. Desserts £1.95-2.15. Booking advised.

Windmill Restaurant

486 Fulham Road, Fulham
London SW6 5NH
Tel: 0171-381 2372 Fax:
Open: Mon-Sat 11.00-23.00. Closed Sun.
Wholefood vegetarian restaurant with heaps of vegan food. 6 entrées £2.50-3.95 like lentil and coconut soup ; Hungarian mushroom soup; organic hoummous platter with red lentil and olive pate with organic wholemeal bread; quesadillas with wild mushrooms (all vegan). 7 salads £1.50-4.25 or have a mixture of all. 3 vegan and 4 veggie dishes daily from a menu. Vegan dishes include brochette of tofu and roasted veg served on coconut and blackeye bean rice plus plantain and chips; sweet potato rosti with red onion gravy and steamed broccoli. Beer £2.25. All wines are organic, some vegan, all are vegetarian, £8.95. Teas 85p pot, coffee £1. Soya milk available. You can bring your own booze £1.50 bottle.

Gardners at 511

511 Fulham Road, Fulham, London SW6 1HH
Tel: 0171-381 1411.
Open: Tue-Sat 17-24.00. Tube: Fulham Broadway
Vegan restaurant with Potager (kitchen garden) cuisine, opened by Michael and Philippa Pettet in 1996. Allow about £15 for three courses. You can have soup of the day, satay,

mezze, pate with their own bread, Spanish tapas, nachos or antipasto for starters. Lots of mains which could for example be potager pie; chilli couscous with grilled vegetables and red pepper sauce; French shepherd's pie; seared and sizzling Viennese minced tofu-steak served with a creamy sauce; fiery hot Tex Mex chilli with rice, salsa, guacamole and refried beans. And now for our favourite bit, a long totally vegan dessert menu: hot devil's food cake, French apple pie with non-dairy ice cream for dessert etc. Drinks are vegan too.

THE CITY

Ravi Shankar's

422 St John's Street, London EC1
Tel: 0171-833 5849 Fax:
Open every day 12-22.30
Famous vegetarian South Indian restaurant in the City, owned by the same folks as the other Ravi Shankar in NW1 and with a similar menu. All 38 dishes are vegetarian specialities from Kerala, including the £6 3-course thali, and only vegetable ghee is used. Bring your own alcohol, free corkage. Booking advised. There's an off-license nearby.

The Greenery

5 Cowcross St, London EC1M 6DR
Tel: 0171-490 4870 Fax: 0171-490 4870
Open: Mon-Fri 07.00-15.00. Closed Sat-Sun.
Excellent wholefood vegetarian café with big take-away trade near Farringdon tube. 50% vegan. Soup £1.15 small, £2.20 large. Filled baps £1.60-1.90. 10 salads daily £1.25-3.00 like pasta, potato, macrobiotic rice, mixed veggies. 3-4 vegan and 3-4 veggie mains £1.80-2.95 like lasagne, Homity pie, curries, pizza, sheperdhess pie, veggie satay, noodles. 3 vegan and 7 veggie desserts, mostly cakes plus fruit salad and trifle. Teas or coffee 60p, with soya milk. They also do breakfast with muesli, croissant, fruit scones, chocolate croissant, toast etc.

Carnevale

135 Whitecross Street, London EC1Y 8JL
Tel: 0171-250 3452 Fax: 0181-336 6322
Open: Mon-Sat 10-22.30, closed Sun.
Vegetarian restaurant, snack bar and take-away specialising in Mediterranean food in the City. 4 vegan and around 8 vegetarian starters £3-4.50. 10 salads £3.75-6.75. 3 vegan and 5 vegetarian mains £6.75-9.00 such as middle Eastern spiced stew with white beans, okra and tomatoes. Olives £1.50. 2 vegan and 7 veggie desserts £3.75 include chocolate brownie tart, fruit compote. 3 course set menu or 2 courses and a drink for £9.50 12-15.00 and 17.30-19.00. Beer, wine from £8.50 bottle, £2 glass. Lots of spirits. Teas £1, coffee £1.20. Soya milk available. Minimum food order £5.50. Cash, cheques or debit cards but no credit or charge cards.

Futures!! Café-Bar

2 Exchange Square, Off Primrose Street
London EC2A 2EH
Tel: 0171-638 6341 Fax: 0171-621 9508
Open: Mon-Fri 07.30-22.00 (Fri 23.00), bar only in evenings.
Big vegetarian café with all types of cuisine that becomes a bar in the evenings. On the edge of Liverpool Street station with slick, modern décor, large conservatory and outside seating. Giant eat-in or take-away breakfast menu from 07.30-10.30am includes home made muesli £1.75 eat in (£1.20 take-away), full cooked brekkies £4.95, pastries, muffins, pot of tea £1.30 (65p) and 6 kinds of coffee. After a work or sightseeing break, pop back for for pastries with morning coffee or afternoon tea. The lunch menu changes monthly with daily specials Tue-Fri. Nibbles £1.50, soup with roll £2.95, side salad £4.50, large salad £6.50, pasta of the day £5.75. Main courses £7 such as red rice with fried aubergines and mushrooms with coconut curry (vegan); sugar snaps, courgettes, babycorn and mange tout served with watercress sauce and duchesse potatoes. Desserts £3.90 include exotic fruit platter or apple and raspberry crumble. Fully licensed, house wine £9.75 bottle, £2.75 glass. No food in the evening, just a busy bar.

The Place Below

Crypt of St Mary-le-Bow Church
Cheapside, London EC2V 6AU
Tel: 0171-329 0789 Fax: 0171-329 0789
Open: Mon-Fri 07.30-14.30
Vegetarian restaurant and take-away. Menu changes daily.
Soup £1.90 take-away, £2.70 inside. Superb salads £4.70 take-away, £7 eat in. Main courses £3.80 take-away, £6.50 eat in, could be potato and aubergine curry with rice and mango salsa; mushroom casserole with olive oil and tahini potato mash. Desserts £2 out, £3 in, like apple and plum crumble.
Bring your own booze £1.50 corkage. Unlimited cappucino, espresso, cofee, tea, herb tea £1.50 between 12 and 2 or £1 at all other times. Available for private hire evenings.

Futures! Vegetarian Takeaway

8 Botolph Alley
Eastcheap, London EC3R 8DR
Tel: 0171-623 4529 Fax: 0171-621 9508
Open: Mon-Fri breakfast 07.30-10.00, lunch 11.30-15.00.
Vegetarian take-away in a secluded pedestrianised alley in the heart of the City. Main course bake, hot pot or savouries £3.40 such as tagliatelle in tomato sauce with spinach and mushrooms; or stir fried veg with rice. Soup £1.75. Salads £1.15 or a combination £2.70. Desserts £1.70 hot or cold such as vegan apple and apricot crumble. Cake 90p. Drinks 45p-£1.20. City tycoons can check the daily menu on Reuters LOLO L852/853 then order by phone. See EC2 for brekkers menu.

Rye Wholefoods

35a Myddleton St, EC1R. Tel: 0171-278 5878
Open: Mon-Fri 09.00-17.30, Sat 10.30-16.00
Wholefood shop with a mini vegetarian café with 12 seats, nearly all vegan. 10 superb vegan salads, pastries, sandwiches, pies, hot and cold drinks. Fill up for £3 or less.

EAST END (JOHN)

The Cherry Orchard

241 Globe Road
Bethnal Green, London E2 0JD
Tel: 0181-980 6678 Fax:
Open: Mon: 11-15.00. Tue-Fri 11-19.00. Closed Sat-Sun.
Vegetarian restaurant East of the City. Start with a vegan soup of the day or oven baked potato £1.60. All salads are vegan 70p-£2.40 such as pasta, olive and pesto; carrot and watercress; tomato and garlic; pink coleslaw or white and red cabbage in vegan mayonnaise. 2 vegan and 2 veggie main courses £2.60-£3.85 could be spicy nacho bean pie and salad; Thai style tofu and veg with brown rice; chick pea and tomato curry with basmati rice. Wide range of homebaked cakes, including vegan, sugar-free and wheatfree (but not cakefree) - and get this, hot vegan apple crumble every day, oh yes. Tea 60p, coffee 90p, soya milk and soya milkshakes. No booze so bring your own and pay £1 corkage. 3 highchairs. Wheelchair access. Discounts for HIV+.

The Thai Garden

249 Globe Road
Bethnal Green
London E2 0JD
Tel: 0181-981 5748 Fax:
Open: Mon-Fri 12-14.45, Mon-Sat 18-2.45
Great Thai vegetarian and seafood restaurant where you'll pay a lot less than in the West End. 33 vegetarian dishes of which many are vegan. 13 starters £3.50-4.00 such as spring rolls, deep fried tempura mushrooms, bean curd, soups. Mains £4-4.50 include bean curd curry with onions, potatoes and peanuts in coconut cream; Thai aubergines and mixed vegetable curry; fried rice noodles with mushrooms and mixed vegetables in black bean sauce. Beer £1.20-2.20. House wine £7.50 bottle, £2 glass. Tea or coffee 80p but no soya milk.

Gallery Café

21 Old Ford Road, London E2 9PL
Tel: 0181-983 3624 Fax:
Open: Mon-Sat 10.30-17.00 (Tue from 12.00), closed Sun
Cosmopolitan vegetarian café run by Buddhists with outside seating in summer. A different home made soup each day such as red lentil and spinach or red pepper and tomato £1.90 or £2.20 with bread. 3 salads daily £1.70-2.80. Dish of the day £3.80 could be vegetable korma, satay or goulash. Selection of home made cakes £1.30, cheesecakes £1.80, pastries from £1. Juices 90p, cuppa 70p, coffee £1, soya milk. Alcohol free. Selection of sandwiches such as focaccia bread with home made pesto sauce and baked vegetables, sunflower topedoes and bagels with various fillings.

Pumpkins

76a Clarence Road, Hackney
London E5 8HB
Tel: 0181-533 1214 Fax:
Open: Mon-Sat 12.00-21.30, closed Sun
Super vegetarian wholefood café-restaurant with remarkably low prices and heaps for vegans. 6 vegan and 3 veggie starters £1-2.25. 6 vegan and 3 veggie mains £3.95-4.95 like lasagne, nut roast, quiche, lentil roast, vegan cheese pie, home made tofu burgers and soups. 3 or 4 salads £1-1.75. Vegan cakes, bakes and cheesecake. Teas 30-50p, coffees 80p-£1.65, soya milk and milkshakes £1.20. Bring your own booze for 40p corkage, off-license nearby.

Ronak Restaurant

317 Romford Road, Forest Gate
London E7 9HA
Tel: 0181-519 2110. Open Tue-Sun 12-22.00, closed Mon
Vegetarian South Indian restaurant still going strong after 20 years. Masala dosa £4, de luxe thali £7.50.

Green Door Café

The Print House
18 Ashwin Street
Hackney
London E8 3DL
Tel: 0171-249 6793 Fax: 0171-503 8034
Open: Mon-Fri 09.00-15.00
Modern world vegetarian and vegan café near Dalston
Junction. Daily soup £1.70. 4 salads £1.50-2.70 like mixed
leaf, pasta in olives and peppers. 1 vegan and 2 veggie main
courses daily £3.20 such as sweet potato satay with rice;
aubergine and sweetcorn pizza; gluten free, vegan pumpkin
coconut stew; vegan vegetable hot pot with leek dumpling;
country pie. Desserts £1.25-1.50 include vegan chocolate and
banana cake. Beer £1.50. House wine £6.95, £1.60 glass.
Teas 70p, coffee 90p, soya milk.

Gannets Café and Restaurant

Hornbeam Environmental Centre
458 Hoe Street
Walthamstow
London E17 9AH
Tel: 0181-558 6880 Fax:
Open: Mon 12-15.00, Tue-Thu 12-15.30. Fri 12-15.30 & 19-
22.00. Sat 10-16.30.
Vegetarian wholefood café and take-away, 50% vegan with
changing menu daily. Starters £2.10-3.75 such as soups, fried
plantain with salsa dip, tortilla chips with chilli bean dip. Vegan
salads £1.50 include tomato, basil and olive; wheat grain
salad. 3 vegan and 2 veggie main courses £3.75-5.95 could
be pasta bake with sundried tomato and broccoli; 5 bean tahini
pie; smoked tofu and mixed pepper korma; spinach and sweet
potato curry. 5 veggie and 5 vegan desserts 95p-£2.25
include fruit crumbles, chocolate cake, pecan pie. Beer £2.50.
House wine £8 bottle, £2.10 glass. Tea 60p cup, £1.20 pot,
coffee 60p, they have soya milk.
Available for private dinner parties and outside catering.

NORTH LONDON

Islington

Bennett & Luck Café

54 Islington Park St
Islington, London N1 1PX
Tel: 0171-226 3422 Fax:
Open: Mon-Fri 9-19.00, Sat 9-18.00, closed Sun
Wholefood shop with a vegetarian and vegan snack bar and
one table, if it's free. Take-away salads and sandwiches.

Milan

52 Caledonian Road
Kings Cross, London N1 9DP
Tel: 0171-278 3812 Fax:
Open: Mon-Sat 12-15.00, 18-21.30, closed Sun
Vegetarian restaurant with North, West and South Indian food.
Eat for a fiver or less. They use sunflower or corn oil, not but-
ter ghee. Great value thalis for £6. Bring your own booze.

Indian Vegetarian Bhelpuri House

92-93 Chapel Market
Islington, London N1 9EX
Tel: 0171-837 4607 Fax:
Open: Every day 12.00-15.00, 18.00-23.00
Vegetarian. Indian. Delicious Indian food at rock bottom prices.
Eat as much as you like buffet for £2.95 in this big place with
all your hungry mates.The only place we know of with vegan
lassi yoghurt drink and a wider range of vegan desserts than
the average Indian restaurant, which usually have dairy everything. The only problem is that after the buffet you may not
have room for one.

Charminar Indian Vegetarian Restaurant

21 Chapel Market, Angel, Islington
London N1 9EZ
Tel: 0171-278 9322 Fax:
Open: Mon-Fri 12-14.30, 18-23.00. Sat-Sun 12-23.30.
Vegetarian Indian restaurant and take-away with much of the menu vegan. Most popular is their seven day all-you-can-eat buffet lunch and evening only for £2.95 (children under nine £1.95) with 25 dishes including rice, starter, salad, desserts, naan bread. Also an a la carte menu including thalis £4.95 and £5.50, dhosas £2.50-3.10, pooris £2.25-2.75. Chef's specialities with rice or nan £3.95 such as vegetable dhansak or jalfrezi Heaps of side dishes £1.80, nans, parathas and rices. Children's vegetable burger with chips, fried mushroom, onion, peas and tomato £1.80. House wine £6.95 bottle, glass £1.50. Tea or coffee 95p, soya milk available and soya milkshakes. Free home delivery over £10 within 3 miles.

Finchley

Mahavir Sweet Mart

127c High Road
East Finchley, London N2 8AJ
Tel: 0181-883 4595 Fax:
Open: Tue-Sat 11-20.30, Sun 10.30-18.30, closed Mon
Indian vegetarian take-away with bhajias, pakoras, garlic potatoes, curries, vegan puris and of course Indian sweets.

Rani Indian Vegetarian Restaurant

3-5 Long Lane
Finchley, London N3 2PR
Tel: 0181-349 4386/2636 Fax:
Open every day 18-22.00. Also Sunday lunch 12.15-14.30 (last order).
Gujarati and South Indian vegetarian restaurant. Average dinner £15 for two courses. Comprehensive menu with specialities changing daily. Dairy and wheat free dishes are marked and they don't use egg, so it's good for vegans. Braille menu.

Finsbury Park

Sunderban Tandoori

50 Blackstock Road, Finsbury Park, London N4
Tel: 01771-359 9243 Fax:
Open every day 12-14.30, 18-24.00
Omnivorous Bangladeshi restaurant with 41 vegan and 53 veggie items. Around £7 if choosing dishes, £8.50 for a thali.

Jai Krishna

161 Stroud Green Road
Finsbury Park, London N4 3PZ
Tel: 0171-272 1680 Fax:
Mon-Sat 12-14.00 & 17.30-23.00, closed Sun
Crouch Hill B/R or Finsbury Park tube.
South Indian and Gujarati vegetarian restaurant with a wide range of veg and vegan starters such as pakoras, dosas, katchuri etc. Mains £4-£5 include with all the usual favourites. Very good value and can get busy, so worth booking on Fri or Sat nights.

Archway

Café Vert

Jacksons Lane Community Centre
269a Archway Road, London N6 5AA
Tel: 0181-348 7666 Fax: 0181 348 2424
Open: Mon-Sat 10-21.00, Sun 12-15.30
Vegetarian café and take-away with a range of international dishes. £1-2.25 gets you vegan bhajias, samosas or a different soup every day, such as leek and potato, lentil with cumin, or pumpkin and tomato. 2 vegan and 2 veggie salads £2.25-3.50. 2/3 vegan and 3/4 veggie main courses like moussaka, nut roast with onion gravy, filled potato skins, Bombay potato pif and many more. Vegan fruit cumble, banana cake, choc cake, vegan fruit bread, Dutch apple pie. Beer £2, tea 60p, coffee 80p, soya milk.

Fiction Vegetarian Restaurant

60 Crouch End Hill
London N8 8AG
Tel: 0181-340 3403 Fax: 0181-340 3655
Email: fiction@crouchendhill.demon.co.uk
Open: Tue-Sun 18.30-00.30, last orders 22.30
Hot new vegetarian restaurant, menu changes monthly. Starters might be soup of the day with bread £3.25; leek profiteroles with sauce £2.95; roast red pepper and almond dip with herb bread £3.50; luxury black truffle paté with lemon stuffed olives and crostini £4.50. Main courses £6.95-8.95 could be Donegal Irish stew with roast seasonal veg cooked in Murphys stout, served with Bundorran sausages; gado gado noodles, mange-tout and baby corn in a spicy peanut and tomato sauce, garnished with fresh coriander and chili nuts and served with sweet potato; wood roasted butternut squash filled with lemon garlic mushrooms, served with Glamorgan sausages, glazed Brussels sprouts and tangy Cointreau and orange sauce; gnocchi a la Romaine. Side dishes £1.25-1.95 like roasted parsnips or mixed green salad. 4 mostly dairy desserts £2.95-3.50 such as three layered chocolate terrine with sherry and blueberry compote or a crumble. Wines from £8.95. Stunning courtyard garden packed out during the summer months. Once a month they do a different topical theme evening on a Saturday with the emphasis on doing vegetarian food in a really amazing way, e.g. the Titanic special went down well in Jan 98. Get a bus W2 or W7 from Finsbury Park tube, get off at the clock tower in Crouch End. Or bus 41 or 91 or N91. Also parties and weddings. Website: www.fiction.mcmail.com

Oshobasho Cafe

Highgate Wood, Muswell Hill Road
London N10 3JN
Tel: 0181-444 1505 Fax:
Open every day except Mon 9-17.00
Completely vegetarian café, average £5 for a meal, in the middle of Highgate Wood, between Muswell Hill and Highgate.

Stoke Newington

Rasa

55 Stoke Newington Church Street
Stoke Newington, London N16 0AR
Tel: 0171-249 0344 Fax:
Open: every day except Mon 12.30-14.00, every day 18-23.00
(Fri-Sat 24.00)
Vegetarian South Indian restaurant that caters well for vegans
as they don't use cheese or eggs at all. Definitely a cut above
most Indians with dishes that are never oily and very fresh.
Try Kappa and Kadala curry, lemon coloured chunks of tapioca
root with fresh curry leaves and toasted spices served with
chick pea curry and fresh coconut. Pal curry features steamed
spongy rice cakes with a carrot and bean coconut stew. Finish
off with vegan kesari, a vegan semolina dessert with cashew
nuts and sultanas. Very popular so book a couple of days
ahead. No smoking throughout. Occasionally closed for
lunch.

NORTH WEST

Manna Wholefood Vegetarian Restaurant

4 Erskine Road, Primrose Hill
London NW3 3AJ
Tel: 0171-722 8028 Fax: 0171-722 8088
Open every day 19.00-23.00
Very classy wholefood vegetarian restaurant with lots of vegan
food. Starters around £4 include Thai aubergine kebabs, tempura mushrooms with tofu, or a mega Manna Meze selection
for £9.75. 6 side or main salads for £3.25-7.75 could be wild
rice with hazelnut and apple salad; caramelised butternut
squash and courgette with red wine and mint vinaigrette; or a
combination. 6 mains for £7.75-8.75 are 50% vegan such as
organic pasta; roast tofu with wasabi, grilled aubergine with
miso, sesame spinach and umeboshi rice; Caribbean hotpot;
or black bean burritos. 5 desserts £3.75 include vegan fruit

crumble with soya cream or baked pears with chocolate sauce. Gallons of hot drinks from £1.20, liqueurs £4.50, OJ 95p, organic apple juice £1.25, or try a Manna coconut milk cooler with fresh strawberries and pineapple £1.95 - better than any mooshake. Lager and organic beer from £2.30. House wine £8.25.

Vegetarian Cottage

91 Haverstock Hill
London NW3 4RL
Tel: 0171-586 1257 Fax:
Open every day 18-23.00
Top class Chinese vegetarian and fish restaurant just down the road from Hampstead village. Best deal is the Sunday 4 course lunch for £8.50. A la carte soups £1.80, starters £2.20, main dishes £4.60. 6 vegan desserts £1.50-2.00.

Kadiris of Hendon

2 Park Road
Hendon, London NW4 3PQ
Tel: 0181-202 2929 Fax:
Open: Tue 18-22.30, Wed-Sun 12-23.00
New Indian omnivorous restaurant with plenty for vegetarians but not vegans.

Geeta

59 Willesden Lane
Willesden, London NW6
Tel: 0171-624 1713 Fax:
Open: every day 18-22.30
Omnivorous South Indian restaurant with lots of excellent vegetarian and vegan food from Tamil Nadu and Kerala at low prices, especially dosas, with coconut a favourite ingredient. Three courses for about £8.

Surya Restaurant
59-61 Fortune Green Rd
London NW6 1DR, Tel: 0171-435 7486 Fax:
Open every day 18-22.30
Relaxed North Indian vegetarian restaurant with dishes from
other parts of India too, including dosas from the South.
Desserts are the usual Indian sweets and vegan halva. On
Sunday they do a buffet lunch 12.00-14.30.

Kanhaiya Sweet Mart
198 The Broadway
West Hendon, London NW9
Tel: 0181-202 4590 Fax:
Open: every day 10-21.00
All vegetarian and vegan Indian sweet shop with take-away
savouries, curry, rice and chappatis. Seating for 12 people.

Rajen's Vegetarian Restaurant
195-197 The Broadway
West Hendon, London NW9 6LP
Tel: 0181-203 8522 Fax:
Open: Mon-Fri 12-15.00, 18-22.00. Sat-Sun 12.00-22.00.
Indian vegetarian restaurant and take-away close to the mega-
crossroads where the M1 meets the North Circular meets the
Edgware Road. Don't miss their speciality eat as much as you
like buffet thali £4.99 at lunchtime or evening. Bargain a la
carte menu £1.95-2.50 per dish, like bhel poori, kachori,
masala dosa, onion uttapam, idli, spring roll. Juices and drinks
from 70p Free car park at the back.

Chandni Sweet Mart

141 The Broadway
West Hendon, London NW9 7DY
Tel: 0181-202 9625 Fax:
Open: every day 08.00-19.00
Indian vegetarian take-away with mostly sweets such as jelabi, barfi, ladu, some of them vegan as they use vegetable ghee.

Gayatri Sweet Mart

467 Kingsbury Road
Kingsbury, London NW9 9DY
Tel: 0181-200 8544 Fax: 0181-205 1872
Open: Mon-Fri 10.30-18.30. Sat 10-19.00. Sun 9-16.00.
Indian vegetarian take-away. 46 dishes £3-4.50 per pound. Savouries like samosa, bhajias, dhokra, kachori. Sweets include barfis, pendas, ladoos, chevda (Bombay mix).

Bhavna Sweet Mart

237 High Road
Willesden, London NW10
Tel: 0181-459 2516 Fax:
Open: every dat 10-21.00
Indian vegetarian and vegan take-away sweets, curries for under £2, naan, parathas, bhajias etc. Don't get there too late in the day in case all the best stuff's been scoffed.

Sabras Indian Vegetarian Restaurant

263 High Road
Willesden Green, London NW10 2RX
Tel: 0181-459 0340 Fax:
Open: Tue-Sun 18.30-22.30, closed Mon.
Vegetarian South Indian and Gujarati restaurant near the North Circular and Edgware Road. The only restaurant to win Best Indian Vegetarian Restaurant of the Year four times, plus lots

of other awards with photos and certificates on display.
Farsan spicy savouries served with chutneys £2.35-2.75 like
samosa, kachori, patra, bhajiyas, patish, moong dal vada, or a
selection of 3 for £3.75 or all 6 for £6.75. Bombay Mumbai
specialities £2,35-3.25 such as bhel puri, sev-puri, pani puri,
dahi vada, ragada patish. 7 kinds of filling dhosas £3.95-6.50,
South Indian pancakes stuffed with potatoes, onions, lentils
and topped with such goodies as cashews, raisins, coconut,
coriander, tomatoes or chilli. 10 Gujarati vegetable dishes
£3.95-4.25 such as Bombay potatoes, special vegetables,
steamed aubergine and petis pois, chick peas and spiced
potatoes in a tangy tamarind sauce. 8 North Indian dishes
£3.95-4.25 are cooked with ground nut oil instead of butter
ghee to make them easier to digest, especially if you're trying
to eat more vegan food, such as chevati dal - four kinds of
split lentils with garlic and spices; black lentils in a fresh ginger,
garlicky tomato gravy; Kashmiri kofta vegetable balls in a nutty
lentil sauce. Mini thalis £5.95, standard thali £9.95, awesome
Sabras thali £14.95, served till 20.00. 11 desserts £2.25-2.50,

some of them vegan. Fresh apple or carrot or both juice
£2.35, lassi, teas, lots of bottled beers £2.35, and of course
wine from £9.95 a bottle, £1.85 glass. Indian champagne
£15.95, French £20.95-24.95.
Famous diners here include Pandit Ravi Shakar, Sir Andrew
Lloyd Webber, Ken Livingstone.

Willesden Sweet Mart

265 High Road, Willesden
London NW10 2RX
Tel: 0181-451 1276 Fax:
Open: Wed-Mon 10-20.00, closed Tue
Vegetarian Indian meals and snacks to take-away with a few
seats to eat in. Some dishes are vegan and all are made on
the premises. Curry and rice for under £3.

WEST LONDON

Bayswater

Kalamaras Restaurant

66 and 76-78 Inverness Mews
Bayswater, London W2 3JQ
Tel: 0171-727 5082/9122 Fax: 0171 2219411
Open: Every day 17.30-24.00, last order 23.30
Two Mediterranean (Greek) omnivorous tavernas in a veggie-
less area on the north side of Hyde Park, close to Paddington
Station. Vegetarians can try lots of starters for £2.60-4.60
such as aubergine dip or fresh artichoke hearts casseroled
with broad beans and dill. House wine £8.50 bottle, £2.50
glass. Tea or coffee £1.50, soya milk available. Discount for
Vegetarian Society members.

Hammersmith

The Gate

51 Queen Caroline St
Hammersmith, London W6 9QL
Tel: 0181-748 6932 Fax: 0181-563 1719
Open: Mon-Sat 18-23.00; also Tue-Fri 12-15.00.
Top class vegetarian restaurant with Mediterranean, Middle Eastern, Oriental, Indian and European cuisine. 2 vegan and 5 vegetarian entrées £3.50-4.80 such as pan-fried potato gnocchi with olives, capers and hazlenut pesto; char-grilled vegetables with parsley and lemon. 1 vegan and 2 veggie salads £3.20-3.50 include Rocket salad with capers, black olives and herbs. 2 vegan and 4 veggie main dishes £6.50-8.50 could be pasta; wild mushroom risotto; aubergine rolls. 2 vegan and 4 veggie desserts such as glazed pear with a chilli anglaise. House wine £8.25 bottle, £1.90 glass. Tea or coffee £1.25, soya milk and milkshakes. Corkage charge £5.

Kensington

Byblos Mezza of Lebanon

262 Kensington High St, Kensington, London W8 6ND
Tel: 0171-603 4422 Fax: 0171-603 4422
Open every day 11.45-23.45
Lebanese vegetarian and vegan set meal at this omnivorous restaurant with about 10 different hot and cold mezze which consist of pulses, hummus, falafel, tabouleh, vegetables, pastries, rice, dolma etc. Beer £2.35 half pint. House wine £8.85 bottle, glass £2.35. Pot of tea £1.65, coffee £1.65. 10% discount to members of Vegetarian or Vegan Society, Viva!, PETA. Also take-away.

Phoenicia

11-13 Abingdon Road, Kensington, London W8 6AH
Tel: 0171-937 0120 Fax: 0171-937 7668
Open every day 12-24.00

Lebanese restaurant with heaps of vegan dishes. 30 vegan and 6 veggie mezze dishes £3-5.70 like hommos, falafel, aubergine dishes, beans. Salads £2.75. 5 vegan main courses £9.50. Beer £2.20. House wine £10.90, £2.90 glass. Tea or coffee £1.75.

Garden Café

at the London Lighthouse, 111-117 Lancaster Road
London W11, Tel: 0171-792 1200 Fax:
Open: Mon-Fri 9-19.00, Sat-Sun lunchtime
Stylishly decorated omnivorous café which always has some veggie meals. The London Lighthouse is a hostel and home to people suffering from AIDS. On summer days the French windows open out onto a peaceful and relaxing garden. Good quality food at very reasonable prices with meals around £4.

Blah Blah Blah

78 Goldhawk Road, Shepherds Bush, London W12 8HA
Tel: 0181-746 1337 Fax:
Open: Mon-Sat 12-15.00, 19-23.00. Closed Sun.
Vegetarian restaurant with eclectic menu that changes every month. 1-2 vegan starters, 6 veggie, £3.95-7.50. 4 vegan and 7 veggie main courses £6.95-7.50. Bring your own booze, corkage 95p.

Maxim Chinese Restaurant

153-155 Northfield Avenue
West Ealing, London W13 9QT
Tel: 0181-567 1719 Fax: 0181-932 7067
Open: Mon-Sat 12.00-24.00, Sun 18.30-24.00
Omnivorous Peking Chinese restaurant in a part of London that doesn't have any veggie restaurants. About 20 mostly vegan dishes which you can mix and match at £2.20-4.80. Vegetarian set menu £12.90 each for two+ people with hors

d'oeuvres, sweet corn soup, prawn flavour crackers, mixed veg, braised bamboo shoots in soya sauce, creamed Chinese cabbage, fried noodles with bean sprouts, dessert. Beer £2.20. House wine £7.50 bottle, £2 glass. Tea £1.20, coffee £1.50. 10% off on take-away.

SARF OF THE RIVER

South Bank

Bengal Clipper

11-12 Cardamom Building, Shad Thames,
Butlers Wharf, London SE1 2YE
Tel: 0171-357 9001 Fax: 0171 3579002
Open: Mon-Sat 12-15.00, 18-23.30. Sun 12-17.00, 18-23.00.
Omnivorous Indian restaurant on London's historic Spice Wharf, in a popular area around the South Bank that has no totally vegetarian eateries, which is why we have to list it. 14 vegan and 19 vegetarian dishes and side dishes £3.15 up to £14.95 for a vegetarian platter. Beer £2.50. House wine £8.95 bottle, £2.50 glass. Tea or coffee £1.75, no soya milk. Corkage charge £4.95.

Meson Don Felipe

53A The Cut, London SE1 8LF
Tel: 0171-928 3237 Fax:
Open: Mon-Sat 12-23.00 (last orders)
Omnivorous Spanish bar with vegetarian tapas snacks like lentils and fresh vegetables, artichoke heart salad, chickpeas with spinach, and deep fried aubergines for around £3. It gets crowded prior to performances at either the Old or Young Vic theatres nearby.

Sopar Thai Restaurant

105 Southampton Way
Peckham, London SE5 7SX
Tel: 0171-703 8983 Fax:

Open: Mon-Sat 18.00-23.00, closed Sun
Splendid little Thai restaurant with heaps of superb veggie
food at half what you'd pay in the West End. 3 starters £2.50
such as spring rolls. Hot and sour salad £4.50. 21 main dishes
£4.50 include exquisitely flavoured curries such as green veg,
mixed veg with oyster flavour sauce. Vegan dessert banana
cooked in coconut milk £2. Thai beer £2.50 bottle, House wine
£6 bottle, glass £2. Tea £1, coffee £2.

Heather's Vegetarian Restaurant

74 McMillan Street
Deptford, London SE8 3HA
Tel: 0181-691 6665 Fax:
Open: Tue-Fri 12-14.30,19-23.30. Sat 19-23.30. Sun 12.30-
15.30,18.30-21.30.
My favourite vegetarian restaurant in London, virtually all
vegan, well worth the trek down to sarf-east London for a
friends' night out. Loads of meat eaters go to this big restaurant in groups as the grub is so awesomely excellent and the
atmosphere great fun. Superb eat as much as you like buffet
£12 which you can go back to as many times as you like,
including desserts. Or select the components separately £3.50
soup, £7.50 plateful, £3.50 dessert. The components being
West African peanut soup, chilled carrot and orange soup,
caramelised onion tart, brazilnut moussaka, Thai chick pea
curry, mixed vegetable couscous and almond, braised Chinse
leek and pumpkin, mushroom and chestnut pie, 8 salads. Not
forgetting the delicous desserts like hazelnut and pear shortbread, nutty chocolate pudding, pecan and maple syrup pie.
Beer £1.95. House wine £6.50, glass £1.95. Tea 70p, coffee
90p, soya milk. You can also bring your own booze, corkage
90p. Smoke free. Closed Mondays. No credit cards. Booking
advisable. Also catering from picnics to weddings.

Googies

19 Greenwich South Street
Greenwich, London SE10 8NW
Tel: 0181-265 5060 Fax:
Open: Mon-Thu 9-20.00, Fri 9-22.00, Sat 9-18.00, Sun 11-18.00
Mostly vegetarian wholefood bistro with meals, sweets, take-aways and cakes. Main meal for around £4. Some outside seating.

Escaped Bistro

141 Greenwich South Street
Greenwich, London SE10 8NX
Tel: 0181-692 5826 Fax:
Open: Mon-Sat 10-22.30, Sun 12-22.30
Brilliant completely vegetarian café with some vegan dishes.

30 dishes that rotate with five on at any one time such as Thai stir-fry noodles. 40% of the food is vegan. Three course meal for around £10. Get there before Peter Mandelson turns Greenwich into another EuroDisney.

The Caffe

306 New Cross Road
New Cross, London SE14 6AF
Tel: 0181-602 1290 Fax:
Open. Mon-Fri 9.00-18.30. Sat 11.00-15.00. Sun closed.
22 seat café. Entrees £2.15 soups, tomato & basil, carrot & coriander, root ginger & ginger, changes daily. Main courses £1.80-3.50 lasgne, pata & tofu, canneloni, spinach & ricotta, Thai curry, blackeye bean casserole, various curries. Desserts £2.50 fruit salad, kulfi, date & apple slice + selection of vegan snacks & cakes. Tea 50p. Unlicensed, bring your own.

Kachans

62a Plumstead High Street
Plumstead, London SE18
Tel: 0181-317 0202 Fax:
Open: Mon-Sat 9-20.30, Sun 12-20.00
Indian vegetarian restaurant and take-away with vegan food, featuring dishes from South India, Gujarat, the Punjab and Bombay.

Mantanah Thai Cuisine

2 Orton Buildings, Portland Road
South Norwood, London SE25 4UD
Tel: 0181-771 1148 Fax:
Open: Tue-Sat 18.30-23.00, Sun till 22.30. Closed Mon.
Thai restaurant in deepest sarf London near Croydon. Starters from £3.20 like sago dumpling, mini vegetable spring rolls. Papaya salad £4.95. Main dishes £5.25-5.95 include pumpkin curry, stir fried beancurd and ginger sauce. Coconut rice pud-

ding £2. Beer £2.35. House wine £7.50 bottle, £2.20 glass. Tea and coffee £1.

Hollyhocks
10 Knights Hill, West Norwood
London SE27 0HY
Tel: 0181-766 8796 Fax:
Open: Tue-Sun 10-17.00. Closed Mon.
Vegetarian tea rooms of yesteryear, close to the A23 London to Brighton road. Pot of various teas 95p, 20p extra for organic. Pot of coffee £1.30. mugs 75p, juices 60-90p. Lots of luscious sandwiches £1.60-2.60, 30p extra for toasted bread, such as smoky vegetarian bacon with avocado; sliced banana with sweet chocolate spread; apple slices, celery, walnuts and raisins in soya mayonnaise. Also toast, teacakes, muffins, oatcakes, cakes, scones, veg sausage rolls, beans on toast, tarts and crumpet. Children's sarnies and cakes from 55-90p. Friday evening buffet once or twice a month £10.50. Bring your own wine £1 per bottle corkage.

Peter Pepper's
60 Morrish Road, Brixton Hill
London SW2 4EG
Tel: 0181-671 5655 Fax:
Open: Mon-Sat 11-23.00, Sun 11-16.00 and 18-22.30
Super vegetarian café-restaurant at the south end of Brixton Hill A23, just before the south circular road. Late vegetarian cooked breakfast or brunch, gourmet main meals from various parts of the world for £5-6. Lots of coffees, juices and bottled beers and wines. This charming, quiet oasis is a blessing in an area dominated by fast food.

Café on the Common

2 Rookery Road, Clapham Common
London SW4 9DD
Tel: 0171-498 0770 Fax:
Open every day 10-18.00

Vegetarian park café with all kinds of food in the middle of Clapham Common, close to the South Circular road. 50% vegan. 10 entrées £2-£3 like rice balls with pepper mayo; sherried mushroom pate; dolmades and tahini sauce (all vegan). 5 salads £1.50-3.50 are all vegan such as mushroom and mange tout, wheatberry, Greek, couscous. 6 vegan and 10 veggie main courses £3.50-5.00 include chick pea roti, pepper frittata, roast veg lasagne, lentil and pumpkin filo rolls. 3 vegan and 6 veggie desserts £1-£2 such as chocolate fudge cake, plum and pear crumble, pineapple and mango upside down cake (all vegan). Heaps of sandwiches £1.20-£2.00. Toast, bagel, crumpets or muffin all 50p. All day full veggie breakfast £3.50. Teas 50p, coffee 70p, soya milk yeah! Bring your own booze, £1 corkage. Open in the evening for large private dinner bookings.

Tea Room des Artistes

697 Wandsworth Road
London SW8 3JF
Tel: 0171-652 6526 Fax:
Open: Tue-Sun 17.30-01.00, restaurant till 23.00. Closed Mon.

Vegetarian and fish restaurant and wine bar, with wholefood and New World cuisine, in the unique ambience of a 16th century barn. Music some nights. Starters like spiced pumpkin soup with French bread £3.75. Mains from £7.50 could be cashew nut, roasted red pepper, leek and winter veg nut roast with baby roast potatoes and bread and onion sauce; chestnut and wild mushroom risotto with cranberry sauce. Desserts £2.95. Alfresco dining in the garden in summer. Booking advised Fri, Sat.

Cafe Pushkar

16c Market Row, Coldharbour Lane
Brixton, London SW9
Tel: 0171-738 6161   Fax:
Open: Mon-Sat 9.30-17.00 (Wed till 13.30), closed Sun
Vegetarian café at the back of Brixton covered market, behind
the tube station. Huge plate of gorgeous vegetarian or vegan
main course with salads for around £5. Vegan cakes, soya
milkshakes, soya cappucino. Lots of papers to read.

Jacaranda Garden Restaurant

11-13 Brixton Station Road, Brixton, London SW9
Tel: 0171-274 9393   Fax:
Open: Mon-Fri 10-19.00, Sat 10-18.00, closed Sun
Omnivorous café with lots of vegetarian food and some vegan,
next to Brixton market and tube station.

The Green Room

62 Lavender Hill, Battersea, London SW11 5RQ
Tel: 0171-223 4618   Fax:
Open: Wed-Sat 19-23.30
Omnivorous international restaurant specialising in top quality
wholefoods with an emphasis on organic produce. 8 vegan
and 13 vegetarian starters from £3. Popular dishes include
potato pancakes, vegetable strudel, crepes asparagus for
£3.50-£7. Desserts around £3. Excellent wine list including
vegan ones. Live music on Fridays.

Wholemeal Vegetarian Café

1 Shrubbery Road
Streatham, London SW16 2AS
Tel: 0181-769 2423 Fax:
Open every day 12.00-22.00
Wholefood vegetarian restaurant serving the classics, nut roast
as well as Thai, Indian and world cuisine. Large vegan selec-

tion. Celebrating its 20th year.   Organic wines and beers.
Smoke free.

Shahee Bhelpoori

1547 London Road
Norbury, London SW16 4AD
Tel: 0181-679 6275 Fax:
Open every day 12-14.30, 18-23.00.
Indian vegetarian restaurant with 100 dishes, many of them
vegan and virtually anything can be made vegan for you.
Starters £1.70-2.90 like vegetable kebab. Green salad £1.
Main courses from £2.75 include dosas. Thalis from £4.95. 15
desserts from £1.30 including vegan ice cream. Beer £1.85
pint, wine £5.50 bottle or £1.30 glass. Tea 60p, coffee 70p,
soya milk available. 10% discount to Vegetarian or Vegan
Society and Viva! Members. On the A23 Brighton to London
road.

Kastoori

188 Upper Tooting Road
London SW17 7EJ
Tel: 0181-767 7027 Fax:
Open: Wed-Sun 12.30-14.30. Every day 18-22.30.
Vegetarian Indian restaurant with African influence offering 60
dishes and vegan goodies clearly marked. 8 out of 10 starters
are vegan such as 3 samosas for £1.50, 5 sev puri for £2.10
or 5 bhajias for £1.95. Curries £2.95-3.75, dosas £2.50-3.50,
thalis £6.25-11.50. Nine Thank family specials £3.50-3.75
such as African style stuffed banana with stuffed mild chillies in
a spicy tomato sauce; green banana curry; green pepper curry
with sesame and peanut sauce. 5 dairy desserts but vegans
will be stuck with fresh fruit (or you could head for Shahee in
SW16 for vegan ice cream!). Wine £7.25 bottle, £2 glass.
Coffee 65p but no soya milk.

Milan Sweet Mart

158 Upper Tooting Road
Tooting, London SW17 7ER
Tel: 0181-767 4347 Fax:
Open: Mon-Tue 11-21.30, Wed-Sun 11-22.00
Indian vegetarian restaurant and sweet centre with over 50% vegan and clearly marked on the menu. 16 starters £1.25-2.00 like bhajias, spring rolls, kachori, puris, patties. 19 mains and curries £2-£3 of which 16 are vegan such as dosas, mushroom curry, stuffed aubergine curry. All the usuals, parathas, nan, dall, pickles. 8 desserts £1.00-1.75, but not a single one is vegan. House wine £6.25 bottle, £1.50 glass. Mango, orange or passion fruit juice £1.50-1.75. Masala tea 75p, coffee 90p. Service not included. Free box of sweets on take-away over £10. Catering for weddings and parties.

Ambala Sweets

48 Upper Tooting Road
Tooting, London SW17 7PD
Tel: 0181-767 1747 Fax:
Open: Mon-Sat 10-20.00, Sun 10-18.00
Vegetarian take-away with Indian sweets, samosas, pakoras and curries; but not vegan.

Tumbleweeds

32 Tooting Bec Road
Tooting, London SW17 8BD
Tel: 0181-767 9395 Fax:
Open: Tue-Sun 18.30-22.30 (last order 21.30), closed Mon
Vegetarian and vegan wholefood restaurant with all kinds of dishes which change daily such as gado gado, broccoli filo parcels, peanut butter croquettes with tahini sauce. Main courses around £6. Usually there's a pancake dish and a curry. Half price children's portions. Wine and organic pilsner.

MIDDLESEX

Edgware

Chai Chinese Vegetarian Restaurant

236 Station Road
Edgware, Middlesex HA8 7AU
Tel: 0181-905 3033 Fax:
Open every day 18-23.00. Also Wed-Sat 12-14.30.
Super new vegetarian Chinese restaurant which specialises in
an astonishing range of soya fake meats plus lots of other
dishes. The ideal night out for both reluctant and avid vegetarians, with over 50 items on the extensive menu. 15 starters
from £2.20 to £5.50 include dim sum seaweeds and veg;
sesame veg-prawns; deep-fried bean curd; mixed hors d'oeuvres of crispy sweet corn, veg-prawns, veg oysters, seaweeds
and spring roll; soups. 7 specialities £5.50-6.00 include crispy
veg duck or pork with pancakes; veg stuffed mushrooms; veg-
eel in soya sauce with tofu and seaweed. 18 other main
courses £3.80-5.50 with rice such as various stir-fried veg;
several veg chicken dishes; crispy shredded veg-beef with
chilli and carrot strips. Only three desserts of toffee apple or
banana £3, or lychees £2.50. Or go for one of the three set
feasts for two or more people from £13.50 to £17.50 per person, all of which contain various fake flesh. There's also a
table with books on vegetarianism and Buddhist philosophy.

Sakonis Restaurant

114 Station Road, Edgware
Middlesex HA8 7AA
Tel: 0181 951 0058 Fax:
Open: Mon-Thu 12-22.00, Fri-Sat 12-23.00, Sun 12-22.30
Vegetarian snack bar, take-away and delivery service with over
100 Indian and Chinese dishes. See Wembley branch for
details.

Satyam Sweet Mart

24 Queensbury Station Parade
Edgware, Middlesex HA8
Tel: 0181 952 3947 Fax:
Open: Mon-Sat 9-19.00, Sun 9-18.00
Vegetarian Indian with take-away snacks only such as
samosas and bhajias.

Harrow

Jhupdi

235 Station Road, Harrow
Middlesex HA3
Tel: 0181 427 1335 Fax:
Open: Sun-Thu 18-22/00, Fri-Sat 18-23.00. Also Tue-Sat 12-14.30.
South Indian vegetarian restaurant and take-away with vegan
food too. Wonderfully extensive menu drawing on the culinary
traditions of the Punjab and East Africa. A starter plus main
course for under £10, and vegan thalis available.

Natraj

341 Northolt Road, South Harrow
Middlesex HA2 8JB. Tel: 0181 426 8903
Open: every day except Wed 10-19.30
Indian vegetarian take-away with plenty of vegan food. Curry
with rice £2.

Kenton

Supreme Sweets

706 Kenton Road, Kenton, Harrow
Middlesex HA3 9QX
Tel: 0181 206 2212 Fax:
Open: Mon-Fri 10-19.00, Sat 9.30-19.00, Sun 8.30-17.30
Indian vegetarian take-away sweets and savouries like bhajias,
samosas, pakoras from 40p. 75% of the items are vegan.
Like many Hindu shops no eggs are used, and they use veg-
etable oil. Catering for weddings and parties.

Gil Sweet Centre

29 King Street
Southall, Middlesex UB1
Tel: 0181 571 2857 Fax:
Open every day 9-21.00
Popular vegetarian Indian café with good honest food at no frills prices. Main meals include masala dosa £3. Soft drinks 50p with food. Southall is the centre of the Sikh community, full of great shops where you can stock up on vegetarian food, spices and clothes.

Shahanshah

60 North Road
Southall, Middlesex UB1 2SU
Tel: 0181 574 1493 Fax:
Open every day except Tue 10-20.00
Punjabi vegetarian and vegan restaurant, take-away and sweet centre. Six starters for £3, main meal £3-4. Counter service and take-away with soya bean burgers. No alcohol.

Shahanshah

17 South Road, Southall, Middlesex UB1 1SU
Tel: 0181 571 310 Fax:
Open every day except Wed, 10-20.00
Vegetarian Indian like the one above.

Wembley

Chetna's

420 High Road
Wembley, Middlesex HA9 6AH
Tel: 0181 903 5989 Fax:
Open: Mon-Fri 12-15.00, 18-22.30. Sat-Sun 13-22.30
Vegetarian Gujarati and South Indian restaurant. Average £5-6. They use vegan-friendly vegetable ghee.

Maru's Bhajia House

230 Ealing Road, Alperton, Wembley
Middlesex HA0 4QL
Tel: 0181 903 6771 Fax:
Open: Mon-Fri 12-20.45, Sat-Sun 12-21.45
Ealing Road is vegetarian heaven, especially at weekends, with enough cafés to keep you going for a month and brilliant prices. Maru's Kenyan Asian cuisine has been a firm favourite with passing shoppers for 20 years with bhajias of course, maize and assorted snacks famous throughout the area. Asian film starts fill up here on pani puri, kachori and vada.

Naklank Sweet Mart

50b Ealing Road, Wembley, Middlesex HA0 4TQ
Tel: 0181-902 8008 Fax:
Open: Mon-Sat 10.30-19.00, Sun 11.30-19.00
Vegetarian Indian take-away with Gujarati sweets and all kinds of savouries, all made traditionally. Tea and coffee 70p

Sakonis

119-121 Ealing Road, Wembley, Middlesex HAO 4BP
Tel: 0181 903 9601 Fax: 0181 903 7260
Open every day 11-23.00
Vegetarian snack bar, take-away and delivery service with an extensive menu of over 100 Indian and Chinese dishes.   Bites £1.20-2.75 such as crispy bhajias, bhel puri, dahi puri, samosas, toasted sandwich, spring roll, soup, crispy mushrooms. Main dishes £2.50-4.00 such as dosas, hot and spicy uttapa sandwich, falafel, vegetable biryani, veg burger and chips, Szechuan noodles, Haka noodles, veg fried rice, sweet and sour veg, American chop suey. Most items can be prepared hot, medium, mild or without onion or garlic on request. Desserts £1.50-2.75 such as rasmalai, shrikhand, exotic fresh fruit shake, gulab jambu. Teas or coffees 90p, fresh juices from £2, no soya milk. Free delivery service 11-20.00 over £10, Wembley call 0181-903 9601 or 1058, Edgware call 0181-951 0058.

Also at 114-116 Station Road, Edgware and 127-129 Ealing Road, Wembley.

Woodlands Restaurant

402a High Road
Wembley, Middlesex HA9 6AL
Tel: 0181-902 9869 Fax:
Open: 7 days for lunch and dinner
Vegetarian Indian restaurant. Big menu with plenty of savouries for vegans. Starters like samosa and bhel poori £1.70-2.25. Dosas £2.50-3.50, a South Indian crepe of finely ground lentils and rice, stuffed with vegetables and served with a lentil soup and coconut chutney. Uthappam lentil pizza £2.75 plus 30p per extra topping. Veg korma curry with cashews and rice £3.95. Thalis £6.25 or £7.25. Steamed, lemon, coconut, bakala or pillau rice £1.50-2.75. Parties welcome.

EAST ANGLIA

CAMBRIDGESHIRE

Cambridge

The Old Rectory
Landbeach, Cambridge
Cambridgeshire CB4 4ED
Tel: 01223 861507 Fax: 01223 441276
2 double en suite, 1 twin £25-35 (as singles),£45-60 also 1
family room.
Tea/coffee and t/v in rooms, also t/v lounge. Historic home furnished with antiques and musical instruments, in secluded grounds with rare breed sheep and donkeys. Bed and breakfast only, though nearby Cambridge has several options.

Arjuna Wholefood Shop
Mill Road, Cambridge
Tel: Fax:
Open: Mon-Sat 9.30-18.00
Big wholefood shop with takeaway vegetarian and vegan food.

Rainbow Vegetarian Bistro
9A Kings Parade, Cambridge
Tel: 01223-321551 Fax:
Open 9.00-21.00 every day.
Rainbow is totally vegetarian, using freshly made food without additives, colourings or flavourings, Gluten or nut free is clearly indicated for those with food intolerances, non-dairy products are available for garlic butter and sandwiches. Breakfasts from £1.25 for crumpets, toast, muesli etc. £3.75 for fry up. Toasted sandwiches £2.45, soup du jour £1.95. Mains £5.45 gado gado (always impresses when I entertain), cous-cous, pasta, African

pot-au-feu, moussaka etc. Baked spuds £3.75-£5.45. Cakes, slice, loaf and Swedish glace from £1.75. Wide selection of tea, coffee, juices, herbal tea, barley cup etc. from 95p.

Wisbech

Stockyard Farm

Wisbech Road Mrs. Bennett. DETAILS REQUESTED
Welney, Wisbech PE14 9RQ
Tel: 01354 610433 Fax:
Open all year except xmas.

£18 1 double, 1 twin £14-£16 pp, tea/coffee, washbasin in rooms, t/v lounge. Proprietor vegetarian, pets welcome. Free range products and vegan options. Near wildlife and wetlands centre. Between Ely and Wisbech on A1101, at north end of village.

ESSEX

Colchester

Brambles Restaurant

St Johns Street
Colchester, Essex
Daytime only

Organic heathfood with vegetarian selection.

Dedham

Dedham Centre Restaurant

Arts & Crafts Centre
High Street, Dedham
Essex CO7 6AD
Tel: 01206 322 677 Fax:
Everyday 10.00-17.00. Closed Mondays from Jan-March.
Vegetarian tea rooms.

The Whalebone
Chapel Road
Fingringhoe, Near Colchester
Essex CO5 7BG
Tel: 01206 729 307 Fax: 01206 729307
Open: Mon-Fri 10.30-15.00, 17.30-23.00. Sat 10.30-23.00. Sun 10-15.00, 19-22.30.

Omnivorous restaurant with a good selection of veggie and some vegan wholefood, French and English dishes from £4.25 to £6.95. Choose from roasted vegetable tartlet, warm fruits and nuts salad, warm avocado salad, herb salad, spicy lentil in roasted pepper, bubble and squeak topped garlic mushrooms, choc and banana pud, melon Granita with liqueur fruits, chocolate and praline slice. House wine £8.50, £2 glass. Tea £1, coffee £1.25.

NORFOLK

Castle Acre

Castle Cottage
Castle Square, Castle Acre
Norfolk PE32 2AT

Not open - Feb

Tel: 01760 755888 Fax:
Small twin

Wholefood macrobiotic/vegetarian bed and breakfast, with dinner on request, in a rural village four miles from the market town of Swafham. All food is vegan.

Castle Acre is set in the outer bailey of a ruined Norman Castle, amidst rolling countryside where the ancient Peddars Way crosses the River Nor. It is a jewel of a village with a green, castle earthworks and ruins. A few minutes down the lane is the ruined Norman Priory, a Cluniac monastery of amazing size and splendour. There are two pubs, tea room and a restaurant, all offering vegetarian fare.

Castle Cottage is in a quiet location, with a garden backing directly onto the great moat of William de Warenne's ruined

Norman Castle, built around 1070 AD. It's a comfortably modernised cottage, with original oak beams and inglenook fireplace in the living room. There is one single room for short or long stays which converts to a small twin bedded room. Single £16 first two nights, then £14. Twin £25 then £23. Evening meal £9. Bicycle hire £3 half day, £5 full day. Morning yoga, Do-In and meditation are free. Healer group on Monday evenings £3.50. Private cooking tuition £10 per session plus evening meal cost. Shiatsu massage 45 mins £15. Healing, counselling, NLP or relaxation/meditation tuition 30,45 or 60 mins £15, £20 or £25.

Red Lion

Bailey Street, Castle Acre
Norfolk PE32 2AG
Tel: 01760 755557 Fax:

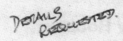

1 double/2 twin £12.50-£15, 1 family £10-12.50, dormitory £10
Vegetarian B&B, originally a pub, meals are communally
served and self catering facilities are available. Table d'hote
dinner, wholefood/vegetarian £7.50, special diets catered for.
Also used for courses, workshops and retreats, has self catering area where visitors can prepare own food or give children
their supper before joining evening meal. The village is in a
conservation area.

Coltishall

Risings

Church Street
Coltishall, Norfolk NR12 7DW
Tel: 01603 737549 Fax:

Omnivorous bed and breakfast with cooked vegetarian and
vegan food in a delightful 17th Century Dutch gable country
home with enclosed garden. One double and two twin rooms,
one of them en suite, £16 per person or £18 in summer. No
evening meal but there are 6 restaurants nearby with veggie
food, including a pub/restaurant The Red Lion next door but
one with a veggie section on its menu.

Diss

Les Amandines

Norfolk House Yard
St Nicholas Street
Diss, Norfolk IP22 3LB
Tel: 01379-640 449 Fax:
Open: Mon and Wed-Sat 10-16.00

Vegetarian and vegan café-restaurant established 12 years, in
the centre of the town, a stone's throw from the old church and
market place. Breakfasts, teas, cakes and lunches.

Fakenham

*

Meadow House

Walsingham Road
Binham, nr Fakenham
Norfolk NR21 0BU
Tel: 01328-830551 Fax:
Open all year

No LONGER IN BUSINESS

Vegetarian B&B situated between the villages of Binham and Great Walsingham, in open countryside, approx 3 miles from the unspoilt North Norfolk coastline with its windswept marshes (not always!), sheltered pinewoods, sand dunes and miles of shingle beach. 2 double rooms £16 per person, both looking out over fields, with tea making facilities, CH bathroom with shower. One double can be booked as single with no supplement. Sitting/breakfast room with a log fire for the exclusive use of guests. Veggie or vegan breakfast with the option of vegan muesli, marg and soya milk. Evening meal £8.50
The bird reserves at Blakeney and Cley are nearby and the sea towns of Wells-next-the-Sea, Sheringham and Cromer are in easy reach. Further afield are Kings Lynn and Norwich.

Norwich

The Tree House Vegetarian Restaurant and Takeaway

14-16 Dove Street
Norwich, Norfolk NR2 4DE
Tel: 01603 -763258 Fax:
Open Mon-Wed 10-17.00, Thu 10-21.00, Fri-Sat 10-21.30. Sun closed.

Vegetarian wholefood café-restaurant with mostly organic food. Most dishes are vegan, and Treehouse have an extensive list of gluten-free, sugar-free, candida diet and nut allergy dishes. Menu changes daily, but included are some examples of dishes. Entrées £2.30-3.15 include: Seasonal vegetable, tomato, and carraway soup £2.30; hummus with salad and bread £2.95; carrot and brazil nut pate with toast & salad £3.15. Several vegan main meals £5.60 or snack meals £4.10 all served with a selection of delicious salads: spiced spinach and chickpeas on rice; mushroom and aduki bean potato topped pie; spiced pumpkin gratin; mushrooms and olives in a rich tomato sauce with pasta. Salad £3.15. Carrot cake £1.85. And now for the vegan desserts: blackcurrant tofu cheesecake £2.60, fruity choc 'n' nut squares £1.60, chocolate banana cake £1.85, chocolate orange tofu cheesecake £2.10, flapjack 75p. (Soya) cream or yoghurt 25p. Highchairs available. 48 seats. Non-smoking.

SUFFOLK

Cavendish

Western House
High Street
Cavendish
Suffolk CO10 8AR
Tel: 01787-280550 Fax:
Open all year.
Tudor house in the middle of the village with spacious garden offering vegetarian bed and breakfast. 1 single £16; 2 twin rooms £32; 1 family room price to be arranged £16 per adult, children half price.Tea/coffee making in rooms. Vegetarian breakfast. Small wholefood shop attached. 20 miles from Beth Chottto's garden at Elmstead.

Ipswich

Marno's
14 St Nicholas Street
Ipswich, Suffolk IP1 1TJ
Tel: 01473 253 106 Fax: 01473 728887
Mon-Fri 10.30-15.30. Thu-Fri 18.00-21.00, Sat 10.30-21.30.
Closed Sun
Vegetarian restaurant and takeaway with good selection of vegan alternatives, international food. Wholefood with special diets catered for. 7 entrees £2.20-3.55, Suffolk falafels, mush-

rooms in cream and basil. 7 Mains £2.75-6.20 with 5 vegan, pan haggerty, various curries, lasagne etc. Vegan and veggie desserts. House wine £7.50.

Woodbridge

Church Cottage
Saxtead, Woodbridge
Suffolk IP13 9QR
Tel: 01728 724067 Fax:
Vegetarian guest house in a 16th century Suffolk rustic cottage with log fires and permaculture. 3 single, 3 double and 1 family room. £15 B & B. No TV or in room facilities. 3 course organic evening meal available using own seasonal vegetables, home made bread and jam. Near the coast, Minesmere bird sanctuary, Snape Maltings and Aldeburgh.

The Old Rectory
Tunstall
Woodbridge
Suffolk IP12 2JP
Tel: 01728 688534 Fax:
1 single £18.50-320, 1 double & 1 twin £35-£38, 1 family £43.75-£57
Open Easter to October. Vegetarian b&b in 2 acre garden in quiet and peaceful Suffolk, evening meal available for £9 by arrangement. Close to Tunstall forest, and the unspoilt Woodbridge, Framlingham and Aldeburgh, with the Maltings only 3 miles for the culture seekers. Seaside towns and some good beaches a short drive away. On B1078 Orford Road quarter mile past church.

HEART OF ENGLAND

BEDFORDSHIRE

Bedford

The Sky's Buffet

9 The Broadway
Bedford
Bedfordshire MK40
Tel: 01234 219 180 Fax:
Open: Every day 12-14.00, 18-23.00
Omnivorous Oriental restaurant with vegetarian and vegan buffet at £5 lunch, £8 evening. From 12-14.00 and after 22.00 you can fill a take-away container from the buffet for £3.   Also veggie and vegan set menu about £6. 3 doors from Kwik-Fit.

BERKSHIRE

Maidenhead

Bradford's Tennis School

Thicket Meadows North
Newlands Drive, Maidenhead
Berkshire SL6 4LL
Tel: 01628-29744 Fax:
Vegetarian bed and breakfast in Edwardian house adjoining National Trust land. 2 double and 1 twin £25-£40. TV in all rooms and washbasin in one. TV lounge. Tea/coffee always available on request. Full English or continental veggie or vegan breakfast with vegan marg, muesli, soya milk and veggie sausages. 10% discount to Vegetarian Society members. If you're into tennis then this is definitely the place for vacations, school holidays or coaching. Vegetarian owner Lionel Bradford was the first tennis professional coach to campaign for nutrition to be included in training and he has researched natural alternative medical treatments for 50 years. He was formerly instructor on the LTA training of teachers scheme and

senior county coach to Essex LTA, the leading county with the highest honours. The three top appointments in British tennis are now held by former pupils. Davis Cup and LTA training. Private lessons £16 one hour, shared £18. Ladies may prefer 45 minutes £13. Private court £5 per hour, tennis machine £4 extra. Informal tennis parties (doubles round-robins) are every 3 weeks at the David Lloyd Club, Heston and indoors at Bucks LTA HQ, High Wycombe, £10, mixed Sunday evenings and ladies Thursday mornings. Tennis memorabilia display of 1,000 items dating from 1900. Raquets and balls at discount prices. Professional advice for new and resurfacing courts. Library of new and secondhand tennis and health books for sale or loan for a token fee.

Highclere

Westridge Open Centre

Andover Road, Highclere
nr Newbury, Berkshire RG20 9PJ
Tel: 01635-253322 Fax:
Open: all year except public holiday periods.

Large country house set in lawned gardens on the lovely Berkshire and Hampshire border, which is an Open Centre for visiting arts and healing studies. This is a comfortable venue for small study groups and a family home for holidays, restful or roaming. Vegetarian owned though not all the food is veggie and they don't recognise special diets or even vegans. 3 single and 2 double rooms £12 per person including breakfast of cereals and unlimited toast. Central heating and washbasins in bedrooms. On weekdays the staff can do cooked breakfasts given notice and can get in things like veggie sausages. Cooked suppers also available if booked for £6. They aim to serve nice people with limited purses like teachers. For added comfort you may want to bring a hot water bottle or use the electric meters for bedroom fires. Also recommended is a torch as there is no street lighting. Smoking permitted in the hall but not the Healing or Recital Rooms or in the bedrooms. Good pub up the road and others in easy driving range, all serving vegetarian meals.

Directions: Highclere is 4 miles south of Newbury on the A343, the Newbury/Andover bus route. Request stop opposite Westridge Studio (the Old Congregational Chapel).
Rail: Paddington/Exeter line to Newbury. Coaches: London Link, and other connections, to Newbury Bus Station. Taxis by arrangement or from Newbury. Walking: the Wayfarers route crosses the A343 near Highclere.

Reading

Cafe Iguana

11 St Marys Butts, Reading, Berkshire
Tel: 0118-9581 357 Fax:
Open: Mon-Thu 11-23.00, Fri-Sat 11-24.00, closed Sun
Vegetarian café which always has something vegan, though not always vegan cakes. Lasagne with massive salad £4.95.
If vegans book dinner they'll make sure you're well catered for.

The Rising Sun

30 Silver Street, Reading, Berkshire
Tel: 0118-9866 788 Fax:
Open: Fri and Sat afternoon and evening
Veggie café in arts centre. When there's a gig on Fri or Sat they're open from about 18.00 till 01.00. Organic beer.
Special Friday night veggie dining occasionally from 20.00.

GLOUCESTERSHIRE

Cheltenham

Below Stairs

103 Promenade
Cheltenham, Gloucestershire GL50 1NW
Tel: 01242 234 599 Fax:
Mon-Sat 12.00-14.30 & !8.00-21.30 closed Sunday
Fish restaurant with at least two vegetarian choices.

The Orange Tree
317 High Street
Cheltenham, Gloucestershire GL50 3HW
Tel: 01242-234 232 Fax:
Open: Mon 10-16.00, Tue-Thu 10-21.00, Fri 10-22.00, Sat 11-22.00,Sun 10.30-15.00

Vegetarian restaurant with vegan, wheat-free and sugar-free food too. Main courses £4.50-7.95. They even have vegan desserts. Fully licensed with organic wines, beers, lagers and ciders. Opposite Zebra health food shop.

Stroud

Mother Nature
2 Bedford Street, Stroud, Gloucestershire GL5 1AY
Tel: 01453 758 202 Fax:
Open: Mon-Sat 9-16.30, closed Sun
Vegetarian café which sometimes has vegan food.

Winchcombe

* ## Hill View Bed and Breakfast
Hill View, Littleworth Nr Greet
Winchcombe, Gloucestershire GL54 5BT
Tel: 01242 603911 Fax: 01242 603639
1 double £17 pp or £20 as single. Own bathroom.

Vegetarian b&b with t/v, tea/coffee in room and sole use bathroom in Victorian house with beautiful views, in quiet Cotswold hamlet. Veg or vegan dinner £10. Good walking country, 84 mile Cotswold Way, Cleve Hill, Sudely Castle, Hailes Abbey, GWR steam railway, Evesham Vale and wonderful unspoilt villages. From Cheltenham take B4632 to Prestbury/Winchcombe. At Winchcombe take 3rd left (North St) after hospital, about a mile and a half take Greet turning on right, Hill View is at bottom of lane on left.Also can be approached from Evesham and Tewkesbury. If lost or confused there's a phone box in Winchcombe and outside the Harvest Home pub on Greet Road.

Wotton-under-Edge

Coombe Lodge

Wotton-under-Edge
Gloucestershire GL12 7NB
Tel: 01453 845057 Fax:
1 single £26-£30, 2 double £40-£46; 1 twin £40-£44, family
£50-£58.50
Vegetarian grade II listed Georgian house in extensive lawned gardens overlooking the Coombe valley offering accommodation in spacious and beautifully furnished rooms with 4 posters, sauna available. T/v and tea/coffee in rooms, also t/v lounge. Bath, Bristol, Cheltenham, Cirencester and Gloucester all about 20 miles. Junction 14 of M5 take B4058, from Wotton war memorial, Coombe Lodge is 1 mile on right.

HEREFORD & WORCESTER

Ewyas Harold

The Poplars

Ewyas Harold
Hereford & Worcester HR2 0HU
Tel: 01981 240516 Fax:
1 single £16-£17, 1 double & 1 twin £32-£34.
Vegetarian b&b Victorian house, washbasins in rooms and t/v lounge. Evening veggie or vegan meal for £14, also packed lunches available. Also French, Spanish and German spoken. Good walking on doorstep as well as pretty little market towns.

Hay on Wye

*

The Old Post Office

Llanigon, Hay on Wye
via Hereford, Hereford & Worcester HR3 5QA
Tel: 01497 820008 Fax:
Open all year
Vegetarian bed and breakfast in a grade II listed building with oak floorboards, beams, antiques and a warm atmosphere. Set in the lovely Brecon Beacons National Park, only two miles from the town of Hay, famous for secondhand books and the book festival for all you J R Hartley fans of yellow`ed pages. One double £15 per person. One double and one twin en suite £20pp. Tea/coffee making in rooms. TV lounge. Veggie brekkers with soya milk and vegan muesli or marg. 10% discount for one week or longer. Good vegetarian choice at Hay restaurants, beautiful walking country.
Directions: From Hay on Wye take the Brecon Rd. After 1/2 mile turn left to Llanigon. Drive 1.5 miles and turn left before school. Old P.O. is white house opposite Church.

Hereford

Harveststore Bistro Café

47 Eign Gate, Hereford
Hereford & Worcester HR4 0AB
Tel: 01432 268209 Fax:
Mon-Sat 9.00-17.00, closed Sun; also pavement café Mar-Oct
Vegetarian wholefood café and take away, starters 70p-£1.90 soup, nutslice, pate etc. Big selection of salads, £2.75, mains £1.80-£3.50 ratatoulle, curry, stews, bakes, baked spuds, sandwiches etc. Desserts 95p-£1.50 fruit salad, soya choccie, bakewell, apple pie. And a 5% discounts for Vegetarian and Vegan Society members.

Nutters

Capuchin Yard, Off Church Street
Hereford, Hereford & Worcester HR1 2LT
Tel: 01432 277 447. Open: Mon-Sat 9.00-18.00, closed Sun.
Vegetarian, soup, jacket potatoes. Mains £4.35-£4.75 nut

roast, pasta, pies, crumble, burgers etc from choice of nine changed daily. Loads of home made cakes and buns 85p-£1.75. Wine £7.50 or very generous glass £1.65.

The Cafe @ All Saints Church

High Street, Hereford
Hereford & Worcester HR2 9AA
Tel: 01432 355088 Fax:
Mon-Sat 8.30-17.45 closed Sun
Vegetarian café which changes menu daily, soup £1.80, quiche with salad or roast spuds £3.75, pasta etc. Sandwiches on own made bread £1.75-£3.45. Desserts £1.75-£1.95. Local beer and cider, also wine £7.95 a bottle.

The Pulse Vegetarian Cafe Ltd

89 East Street, Hereford, Hereford & Worcester HR1 2LU
Tel: 01432 268 473 Fax:
Lunchtimes Mon-Sat 9.00-17.00 Sun 10.00-15.00 also Fri night
20.00-23.30
Occasionally open on Saturday nights for cabaret, parties and theme nights, Friday has a 5 course meal with live band. Worth a call to see if open in evening as fairly new and may have extended evening openings. 90% vegan, offering a hearty breakfast menu. Daytime, selection of starters £1.95-£2.30 soup, hummous, pate. Salads, marinated greek veggies, falafalel, flans, quiche etc. Fun and funky 5 course dinner on Fri night with live music for around £15 pp. No license so bring your own.

Ledbury

Munsley Acre Country House

Mansley, Ledbury
Hereford & Worcester HR8 2SD
Tel: 01531 670568 Fax:
Mainly vegetarian guest house with one vegetarian proprietor, peacefully situated in large gardens on a quiet lane about 4 miles from the small Herefordshire market town of Ledbury. With views all round and with a reputation for a warm welcome, good food and comfortable accommodation. Proprietor Ann Brazier has been vegetarian for over 25 years and specialises in providing delicious, varied and interesting home made vegetarian food. Double or twin £40, second night £34, child sharing £12. Single £25. Evening meal £12 for 3 courses, £8 for one. Group rate £27.50 per person for dinner, bed and breakfast for 2 nights or more. No smoking. Directions: about 1.5 miles along a quiet back-road off the A438 towards Hereford.

Malvern

Brief Encounter

Great Malvern Railway Station
Imperial Rd, off Avenue Rd
Malvern, Hereford & Worcester WR14 3AT
Tel: 01684-893033 Fax:
Open: Thu-Sat only 19-23.00
Vegetarian restaurant. 1 vegan and 2 veggie entrées £2.65-2.95 such as spinach pancake roll with fresh chill marmalade. 1 vegan and 3 veggie main dishes £6.25-6.95, for example gingered cashew risotto with an Indonesian peanut relish, served with a mixed salad. 3 desserts (none vegan) £2.95 include cranberry syllabub. Beer, house wine £6.95 or £1.30 glass. Pot of tea 90p, coffee £1.30, no soya milk. 10% discount to Vegetarian Society members.

St Annes Well Cafe

Victoria Walk, St Annes Road
Malvern, Hereford & Worcester WR14 4RF
Tel: 016845 60285 Fax:
Open: Easter-Oct 10-18.00, Winter Sat-Sun only 10-17.00
Vegetarian café with mostly vegan menu.

Ross on Wye

Oat Cuisine

47 Broad Street, Ross on Wye
Hereford & Worcester HR9 7DY
Tel: 01989 566 271 Fax:
Mon-Fri 8.00-18.00. Sat 8.00-17.00. Sun 11.00-16.00.
25 seat vegetarian café & takeaway with wheelchair access.
Entrees £2.25, Salads half-£1.30 full £2.60, 7 main courses
include lasagne, pasties, pizzas, 6 desserts carrot cake,
brownies. Tea/coffee 70p, bring your own booze. Discount for
Vegetarian and Vegan Society members.

HERTFORDSHIRE

Berkhampstead

Cook's Delight

360 High Street
Berkhamsted, Hertfordshire HP4 1HU
Tel: 01442-863584 Fax:
Open: Mon-Sat 9-17.00, closed Sun
Very nice organic wholefood shop with take-away vegan and
vegetarian food, plus heaps of gorgeous Malaysian food in the
freezer. The only place for veggies for miles. If you've come a
long way and let them know, then you could have a light lunch
snack with the staff in the old vegetarian restaurant section.
(There used to be a great veggie restaurant here, but the
Malaysian cook is taking a sabbatical.)

Ware

Sunflowers Restaurant

7 Amwell End
Ware, Hertfordshire SG12 9HP
Tel: 01920 463 358 Fax:
Mon-Fri 8.00-17.50, Sat 9.00-17.30 closed Sun plus monthly
themed monthly.
Vegetarian café and take away in wholefood shop. Home
made soups £1.25, Salad selection, mains around £2.25
spinach pie, pasta, chillie, bakes and jacket potatoes. Fruit and
vanilla dessert, apple pie, ice creams and lots of lovely cakes.
Licensed and you also get a discount in the shop if you are a
VSUK or Vegan Soc member.

Watford

Mavis Tyrwhitt

26-28 Garston Drive
Garston, Watford
Hertfordshire WD2 6LB
Tel: 01923 670478 Fax:
2 single and 2 twin £15 pp per night.
Veg breakfast available in veggie friendly bed and breakfast.

OXFORDSHIRE

Oxford

Cotswold House

363 Banbury Road
Oxford, Oxfordshire OX2 7PL
Tel: 01865 310558 Fax: 01865 310558
Open all year except 10 days at Christmas
Omnivorous guest house run by two vegetarians who will
promise you a decent full English veggie or vegan breakfast.
All rooms are en suite with fridges, tea/coffee making, TV and
more. 2 singles £39-42, 2 doubles and 1 twin £58-62, 2 family
rooms £70-82. Use the ring road, just off A40.

Cafe M.O.M.A. (Museum of Modern Art)

30 Pembroke Street, Oxford, Oxfordshire OX1 1BP
Tel: 01865 722733 Fax:
Open: Tues-Sun 9.30-17.30. Closed Mon.
Omnivorous wholefood café with vegetarian staff. Entrees: e.g. baked filled potatoes £2.30+, filled toasted bagel £2. Main courses e.g. lentil curry, rice, pappadum & minced chutney £3.85, mushroom and courgette loaf & two salads £4.25. Desserts e.g. carrot cake, fruit salad, fresh scones, biscotti. Beer and wine £1.75. Tea 65p, coffee 95p. Non-smoking. 10% discount to Vegetarian and Vegan Society members.

Maya's Restaurant

103 Cowley Road
Oxford, Oxfordshire OX4 1HU
Tel: 01865 722 955 Fax:
Open: lunch Tue-Sat 12-14.00, dinner Mon-Sat 18.30-23.00.
Closed Sun.
Omnivorous restaurant with a menu that's half vegetarian in a town with not much in the way of totally veggie places. Pizza, pasta, salads, aubergine dishes, but no vegan ones. You'll need to book for the evenings, especially at the weekend.

SHROPSHIRE

Bridgnorth

Quaints Vegetarian Bistro

69 St Mary's Street
Bridgnorth, Shropshire WV16 4DR
Tel: 01746 768 980 Fax:
Open: daytime except Mon 10.30-15.00 (Sat -16.00), evening
Tue-Sat 18.30-21.30
Vegetarian bistro slightly marred by a couple of fish dishes. 4 vegetarian and 6 starters and they usually have 1 or 2 vegan dishes but it's best to check.

Church Stretton

Acorn Wholefood
Restaurant & Coffee House

26 Sandford Avenue
Church Stretton, Shropshire SY6 6BW
Tel: 01694 722 495 Fax:
Mon & Thu-Sat 9.30-18.00, Sun 10.00-18.00. Wed on school
hols only, closed Tues.
Offering scones and cakes with teas, coffees, juices, cordial
and de-cafs. Soup and bread £2, nut roast, quiche, pizza, pitta
sandwich, baked spuds, ploughmans £1.75-£3.95. Also alas
meat/fish dish of day.

Ironbridge

Olivers Vegetarian Bistro

33 High Street, Ironbridge
Shropshire TF8 7AG
Tel: 01952 453 086 Fax: 01952 882961
Tue-Thu 19-21.30, Fri-Sat 19-22.00. Also Sat 12-15.00, Sun
11-17.00. Closed Mon.
All day veggie breakfast, Starters £2.45 garlic mushrooms,
potato dippers, soup. Main courses £5.95 nutty stuffed sweet
peppers, pasta fungi gratin, cashewnut & carrot nut roast.
Desserts £2.45 pear & blackberry crunch, summer fruit crum-
ble, chocolate & malibu mousse.

Shrewsbury

The Goodlife Wholefood Restaurant

Barracks Passage, Wyle Cop
Shrewsbury, Shropshire SY1 1XA
Tel: 01743 350455 Fax:
Mon-Sat 9.30-16.30 Closed Sun
Vegetarian wholefood restaurant and coffee shop in one of his-
toric Shrewsbury`s passageways. Fresh food, homemade
cakes. Soup £1.95, Nutloaf or jacket potatoes £1.90. 4 hot

dishes of day £2.25 curry, moussaka, stroganoff, broccoli & hazelnut bake. Salad bar 80p-£2.25, desserts £1.20-£1.80 good vegan selection.

STAFFORDSHIRE

Hanley

Dylans Vegetarian Restaurant

99 Broad St, Hanley, Nr Stoke on Trent
Staffordshire . Tel: 01782 286 009
Mon-Thu 12.00-14.00, 18.00-22.30, Fri till 23.00,
Sat 12.00-21.00, Sun closed

8 starters £2.95 3 vegan, 9 mains £7.95 with mixed veg or salad pepper lasgne, stir fried tofu, chickpea hot pot, 5 vegan options. Desserts £2.95 fresh fruit salad, banana split, chocnut layer. Also childrens menu, lunchtime snacks and sandwiches. Good selection of beers. 15% discount for members of Vegetarian and Vegan Societies, take your membership card.

Rugby

Summersault

27 High Street, Rugby
Warwickshire CV21 3BW
Tel: 01788 543 223 Fax:
Mon-Sat 9.00-16.30 Closed Sunday

75 seat vegetarian restaurant. Entrees from £2.10, range of vegan and vegetarian salads from 70p for side portion. Vegan and vegetarian mains from £3.60, menu changed daily. Selection of desserts £1.40-2.25 all wholemeal. Vegetarian beer £1.50 and wine £1.50 a glass, £6.95 bottle, tea/coffee/herbal tea from 85p.

Stoke-on-Trent

The Rising Sun Inn

Knowle Bank Road, Shraley Brook, Audley
Stoke on Trent, Staffordshire ST7 6DS
Tel: 01782 720 600 Fax:
Pub with own brewery, offering vegeburger and banger bar
snacks £4-£4.50, also gratin, chilli, casserole, lasagne, fettucini
£7.50 including chips, veg or salad. Do try their beers.

WARWICKSHIRE

Stratford on Avon

Parkfield Guest House

3 Broad Walk, Stratford on Avon
Warwickshire CV37 6HS
Tel: 01789 293313 Fax:
Omnivorous guest house. This charming Victorian house is
just a few minutes walk from the centre of town. Vegetarian
B&B with 7 rooms of which 5 are en suite, £18-£21. Wholefood
veggie breakfast.

Winton House

The Green, Upper Quinton
Stratford on Avon, Warwickshire CV37 8SX
Tel: 01789 720500. Lyong@ibm.net
Open all year
Omnivorous historic farmhouse with 1 double, 1 twin, 1 family
all en suite from £48. Tea/coffee in rooms, tv lounge.
Vegetarian breakfast available. From A3400 south Stratford
right onto B4632 for 6 miles then left into Upper Quinton.

Stratford Health Food Cafe

Unit 1, Greenhill Street
Stratford upon Avon, Warwickshire CV37 6LF
Tel: 01789 415 741 Fax:
Mon-Sat 9.00-16.30
Vegetarian wholefood with snacks, cakes, buns etc. Hot
lunches from 11.30-14.15.

Warwick

Park House Guest House

17 Emscote Road, Warwick
Warwickshire CV34 4PH
Tel: 01926 494359 Fax:
Veggie friendly B&B with 8 rooms, all en suite, £17.50-£25.

WEST MIDLANDS

Birmingham

London Sweet Centre

104 Soho Road, Handsworth
Birmingham, West Midlands B21
Tel: 0121 554 1696 Fax:
Small selection of samosas, spring rolls and curry, lots of
sweets though.

Milan Sweet Centre

238 Soho Road, Handsworth
Birmingham, West Midlands B21 9LR
Tel: 0121 551 5239 Fax:
Every day 10.00-19.45
Indian vegetarian.

Milan Sweet Centre

191 Stoney Lane, Sparkhill
Birmingham, West Midlands B12 8BB
Tel: 0121 449 1617 Fax:
Open everday 9.00-20.00.
Indian vegearian takeaway, Entrees are sold by weight £2.00
per pound, various pakoras, samosas, veg cutlets, potato
tikki`s. 10 main courses at £2.00 per portion. Large selection of
Indian sweets.

Pritam Sweet Centre

291 Rookery Road, Handsworth
Birmingham, West Midlands
Tel: 0121 551-5626 Fax: 0121 5540444
Every day 9.30-19.30
Indian vegetarian take away, offering potato & aubergine, pota-
to & cauliflower, chick pea etc. curries. Chappatti`s, naans,
bhaturas (fried naan) and rice.

The Warehouse Cafe

54 Allison Street, Digbeth
Birmingham, West Midlands B5 5TH
Tel: 0121 6330261 Fax:
Open Mon-Sat 12.00-21.00. Open Sunday by arrangement.
Vegetarian restaurant. 85% vegan, including all salads, ice
cream and burgers. Varied menu with a mixture of Indian,
Mediterranean, Mexican, organic, Spanish, Thai, wholefood.
Daytime menu £2.85-3.40 (all served with salad) include
peanut & fresh coriander fritters; peanut and tomato lattice pie
& apple sauce; herb or chilli or savory tofu burger & salad;
falafel. Evening menu specials (all with salad) £5.75-5.95 such
as North African Tagine; leek and cashew nut crispy loaf;
casheu nut paella; Mexican taquitos; aubergine and sweet
potato korma with naan. Vegan desserts £1.50-2.15 e.g.
Amazon trifle, pecan pie, carrot cake, chocolate gateau,
banana split. Bring your own booze with free corkage. Teas
65p, coffee 70p, soya milk and soya milkshakes available.

Discounts for NUS, UB40, OAP, and FoE members. 40 seats.
Chidren's portions and highchairs.

Selly Oak

Wild Oats
5 Raddlebarn Road, Selly Oak
West Midlands B29 6HJ
Tel: 0121 471 2459 Fax:
Tue-Sat 12.00-14.00 & 18.00-21.00
Vegetarian restaurant.

EAST MIDLANDS

DERBYSHIRE

Bakewell

The Cottage Tea Room

3 Fennel Street
Ashford-in-the-Water
Bakewell
Derbyshire DE45 1QF
Tel: 01629 812488 Fax:
Sat & Sun 10.30-12.00 14.30-17.00, Mon,Wed & Thu 14.30-
17.00 closed Tue & Fri

Vegetarian traditional tea rooms on the old Roman road in an unspoilt conservation area in this exquisite Peak District village. They have lots of teas and herbals, with six variations of afternoon tea including a pot with a slice of cake. The accent is on home cooking with traditional English cakes, hand kneaded breads and scones. The cottage is 2 miles north of Bakewell and 8 miles south of Buxton Spa, just above the ford by the sheepwash bridge.

Buxton

Foxlow Grange Vegetarian Guesthouse

Harpur Hill
Buxton, Derbyshire SK17 9LU
Tel: 01298 24507 Fax: 01298 73011

Impressive stone built Georgian fronted farmhouse offering an elegant and spacious oasis of peace. King size room with king size bed £32 per person. Double and twin £27 per person. Lovely cooked breakfast is included with vegan or any other diet catered for. Optional evening meal Fri-Sat £21.50 with four courses freshly prepared. Wine from £7. (Other days you can get veggie food at The Wild Carrot in Buxton.) The Cordon Vert trained proprietor offers a truly home-made and often organic menu, and her husband is a homeopathic doctor,

but please make an appointment.   No children. No pets. No smoking in the building or grounds.
Directions: off Ashbourn A515, one mile from Derby.

Glenwood Vegetarian & Vegan Guest House

134 Lightwood Road
Buxton, Derbyshire SK17 6RW
Tel: 01298 77690 Fax:
1 single £15.50-£17.50, 1 double and 1 family £16.50-£18.50
Tea/coffee and washbasin in rooms, tv lounge. Veg or vegan breakfast and evening meal. Dinner £8 for 2 courses or £10 for 3 - go on treat yourself, have the dessert. In the less crowded Peak District close to Buxton Spa, summer festivals, Chatsworth and Haddon Hall. Lightwood Road is off the A6 to the north east of the town centre, only 10 minutes walk from the railway station.

The Wild Carrot

Just Shop (Sep '04)

5 Bridge Street
Buxton, Derbyshire SK17 7AD
Tel: 01298 22843 Fax:
Wed-Sun 12.00-15.00, 17.30-23.30, last orders 21.30
Vegetarian wholefood café and restaurant. Lunchtime soup, houmous, falafalel, paté, burger £1.50-£1.90. Baked spuds £1-£1.60. 2 main courses for £3.20 with side salad or £4.20 with full salad. Dinner offers 2 starters £2.80; 3 mains £5.25-£5.50 such as bobbotie, tortilla, tagliatelli; and 2 desserts £3.20, vegan option or adaption not a problem. Menu changes monthly. Also happy hour 17.30-18.30 Mon-Fri with £1.50 off main course.

Chesterfield

The Natural Choice Cafe

2/6 Long Shambles
Chesterfield, Derbyshire S40 1PX
Tel: 01246 558 550 Fax: 01246 558550
Mon-Sat 9.00-17.00 closed Sunday.
Veg café and health food shop in Chesterfield, famous for its twisted church spire. Full cooked breakfast 99p Mon-Fri only. Also afternoon tea 99p with scone, cookie or toasted teacake. Various sandwiches and jacket potatoes. Soup or paté from £1.95. Selection of salads for up to £4.50. Mains £2.15-£5 with assorted vegan pasties, pies, casserole, savoury roasts, quiches etc. Heaps of cakes and desserts suitable for diabetics and vegans. Menu changes daily.

Derby

The Incredible String Bean Café

88 Abbey Street
Derby, Derbyshire
Tel: 01332 298 185 Fax:
Mon-Fri 12.00-15.30 closed Sat and Sun
Vegan wholefood café in downtown Derby. 3 different salads 70p-£2 tabouli, green, pasta salad. Choice of 2 mains £1.25-£3 curry, sausage pie, lasagne etc. Dessert apple crumble, chocolate cake. Unlicensed.

Holymoorside

Aaren House

35 Holymoor Road
Holymoorside, Derbyshire S42 7EB
Tel: 01246 566925 Fax:
2 single £17, 2 double & 1 twin £34, 1 family £40-£45
Homely cottage décor with large rooms run by veggie owner. Evening veg or vegan meal £6, in Peak District with all it`s attractions, Sheffield and Chesterfield nearby if you are pining for some nightlife.

LEICESTERSHIRE

Birstall

Dodgy Dick`s Backpackers Hostel

157 Wanlip Lane
Birstall, Leicester
Leicestershire LE4 4GL
Tel: 0116 2673107 Fax:
1 twin £8 and 5 bed dormitory £8
Hostel catering for cyclists, backpackers and students only in a suburban house . Light breakfast or full English £2. Supper £4 which can be veg if requested. Nearby Leicester has squillions of Indian restaurants. 3 miles north of Leicester on A6 or just off M1/A46 junction via Wanlip village.

Leicester

Bobby's

154 Belgrave Road
Leicester LE4 5AT
Tel: 0116 266 0106 Fax:
Open: Mon-Thu 11-22.00, Fri-Sun 11-22.30
Indian vegetarian restaurant with some vegan curries and cha-patties.

Chaat House

108 Belgrave Road
Leicester
Tel: 0116-2660 513 Fax:
Open: Wed-Mon 12-20.15 last order. Closed Tue.
Indian vegetarian restaurant. There is no such thing as bad Indian food in Leicester which has curry houses everywhere. However there is such a thing as outstanding Indian food which you'll find here being munched by the local vegetarian Buddhists, Hindus, Sikhs and vegan Jains.

Currant Affairs
9A Loseby Lane
Leicester LE1 5DR
Tel: 0116 2510887 Fax:
Mon-Sat 9.00-17.30 closed Sunday
Wholefood shop and take away with an emphasis on using organic ingredients. Savouries and cakes all baked on premises.

Mirch Masala
Belgrave Commercial Centre
Belgrave Road, Leicester
Tel: 0116-2610 888 Fax:
Open: Mon-Sun 11.30-22.00, Sun 12-22.00
Indian vegetarian restaurant.

Pizza Pride
21 Melton Road
Leicester
Tel: 0116-2669 522 Fax:
Open: Mon-Fri 11-23.00, Sat 12-22.30, Sun 16-22.30
All vegetarian pizza, pasta, chips, burgers, baked potatoes, but vegans may be literally cheesed off.

Sayonara Thali Restaurant
49 Belgrave Road
Leicester LE4 6AR
Tel: 0116-266 5888 Fax:
All week 12.00-21.30, Sat till 22.00
Indian vegetarian restaurant and take away. Choice of 50 starters from £2.25, all the usual mains and a special thali for £6.95. Various ice creams and indian sweets. Also 10% discount for students.

Sharmilee Restaurant

71-73 Belgrave Road
Leicester LE4 6AS
Tel: 01162 610503 Fax: 01162 681383
Tues-Thurs 12.00-14.30 & 18.00-21.30, Fri-Sun 12.00-21.30,
closed Monday.
Indian vegetarian restaurant and take away. All the usual
favourites.

Sonal's Bhajiya House

122 Narborough Road
Leicester LE3 0BT
Tel: 0116-2470 441 Fax:
Open: Wed-Mon 12-22.00, closed Tue
Vegetarian Indian restaurant with vegan food too. Next to
Barclays bank.

The Landing Vegetarian Restaurant

The Ark Environment Centre
2-6 St Martins Walk
Leicester LE1 5DG
Tel: 0116 251 9022 Fax:
Mon-Fri 10.00-17.00. Sat 9.30-17.00, 19.30-24.00 Closed Sun
Vegetarian and vegan daytime buffet, table service Saturday
nights. International cuisine with organic ingredients. Entrées
£1.95-3.50 such as potato latkes with apple sauce, tapas,
soups. 4 salads £1.85-2.95. Mains £5.95 could be cottage pie,
leek & mushroom casserole, Mediterranean soufflé. Desserts
£1.10-2.95 like vegan chocolate, fresh fruit crumbles, trifles.

The Whole Truth

Belvoir Street
Leicester
Friendly alternative vegetarian café with tasty food. They have lots of theatre leaflets. It's arty but not pretentious, the sort of place you could take your parents and know they'd enjoy it.

Bread & Roses Café and Alhambra Restaurant

70 High Street, Leicester LE1 5YP
Tel: 0116-2532 448.
Open: Café Mon-Fri 12-14.30, Sat 10-17.00.
Restaurant Tue-Sat 18-23.00.
Bread & Roses is a nice little café in the basement of the Alhambra restaurant which has vegan Mediterranean food, perfect for a cuppa with a slice of cake or some other snack in between shopping. The very friendly proprietor cooks all the food himself.
The Alhambra restaurant on the ground and first floors serves Arab and Middle Eastern food which is great for flesh free feasting.

NOTTINGHAMSHIRE

Nottingham

Maxines Salad Table

56-58 Upper Parliament Street, Nottingham NG1 2AG
Tel: 0115-9473 622
Open: Mon & Sat 8.45-17.00, till 19.00 Tue-Fri.
Sun 8.30-15.00.
Vegetarian café offering breakfasts, vegan quiche, cakes etc.

Out To Munch

15 Goosegate
Hoxley, Nottingham NG1 1FE
Tel: 0115 948 1115
9.30-16.00 everyday.
Vegetarian café.

Salamander Restaurant

23/25 Heathcote Street
Hockley, Nottingham NG1 3AG
Tel: 0115-941 0710 Fax:
Mon-Sat 18.00-22.30, Sun 13.00-15.30 & 18.00-21.00
Closed Wed
Vegan gourmet restaurant in lively Nottingham. Entrées £1.95-
£2.75 include tofu & tempeh crunchies; spinach, lentil & apricot
vol au vents; deep fried seaweed etc. Mains £6.45-£7.50 like
stuffed lumaconi, aubergine provencale, rosti layer, brazil nut
en croute; side salad served with all meals. There are 6 vegan
desserts £2.25-£2.75 such as margherita cheesecake, chocolate & hazelnut filo, brandy & prune tartlets. House wine £6.90.
10% discount for Vegetarian Society, Vegan Society, Animal
Aid, PETA and Viva! members.

The Vegetarian Pot

375 Alfreton Road
Radford, Nottingham NG7 5LT
Tel: 0115 9703333 Fax:
Mon-Sat 11.00-14.00, 17.00-21.00 Closed Sun
Vegetarian Indian restaurant and takeaway. Mains £2.25-250,
daily special £2.80, rice £1.50. Thali £3.80-5.80

Veggies Burger Stall

c/o Veggies Catering Campaign
180 Mansfield Road, Nottingham NG1 3HU
Tel: 0115-9585 666 Fax:
Look out for Veggies' bargain mobile burger stall in Clinton Street West in the town centre at lunchtime.

Croft Hotel

6-8 North Road
West Bridgford
Nottinghamshire NG2 7NH
Tel: 0115 981 2744 Fax:
8 single, 6 double, 2 family £15-£25
Veg friendly, breakfast only but not a problem with nearby Nottingham's nightlife and restaurants.

Wellow

Durham Ox

Newark Road
Wellow
Nottinghamshire NG22 0EA
Tel: 01623 861026 Fax:
17th century coaching inn with vegetarian menu for lunch and evening. £4.50 for main Thai stir fry, broccoli bake, lasagne etc. Also a resident ghost apparently.

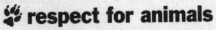

NORTH WEST

CHESHIRE

Altrincham

The Greenhouse

41/43 Oxford Rd,
Altrincham, Cheshire WA14 2ED
Tel: 0161 929 4141 Fax:
Open: Mon-Sat 8.30-17.00. Also Thu-Sat 18-22.45. Closed
Sun.
Vegetarian restaurant. During the day run as a self service restaurant, with 8 salads, 4 flans, spuds, paté, soup and hot dishes of day around £3, or a good lunch for £5-7. In evenings a la carte menu, candle light, waitress service, light jazz background music. £12-£15 for a 3 course meal. Main courses around £8, starters £3.   Always 2 vegan starters and 2 vegan main courses. 2 vegan desserts and another that can be adapted, including fruit in Cointreau or sorbets. There's an early bird special from 6-7pm with 2 courses for £7.50 or 3 for £10. Good selection of vegetarian and vegan wine. Near the headquarters of The Vegetarian Society.

Knutsford

Dick Willett`s

The Toft, Toft Road
Knutsford, Cheshire WA16 9EH
Tel: 01565 633470 Fax:
Family run two star hotel in a converted dairy farm dating back to the 16th Century offering quality rooms and a renowned vegetarian restaurant on the premises. £19.75 for a 4 course dinner freshly prepared and presented by Jean their t/v chef.

GTR MANCHESTER

Chorlton on Medlock

Fallen Angels

263 Upper Brook Street, Chorlton on Medlock
Greater Manchester M13. Tel: 0161-273 4327
Open: Tue-Fri 12-14.00, Tue-Sat 17.30-20.30.
Sun 13.00-19.30.

Vegetarian restaurant which can make dishes vegan, such as garlic bread made with vegan marg. Low cost lunch menu £3.50 could be curry with rice and carrot salad, veg and bean stew with dumplings and bread, bake of the day with potaotes and salad or veg, pasta with salad. Or eat light for £2.50 with garlic mushrooms with French bread and salad, dip of the day with bread or tortilla chips and salad, mixed salad with a basket of bread, big bowl of soup with bread.

In the evening they go up market. 8 starters £2.45-3.25 such as garlic mushrooms; soup, salads, garlic bread, nachos, vegan nachos, dip of the day. 7 delicious main courses served with potatoes or rice and salad or veg £7.45-7.75 include aubergine steaks with peppers and tangy basil sauce; Mexican beanfeast; Fallen Angels curry; grilled polenta with courgette and sun-dried tomato sauce; bake of the day; pasta of the day; stir fry with wheat noodles or rice. Extra side salad £2.75. Desserts £2.95-3.25 are chocolate truffle torte, banoffi pie, char grilled pineapple in ginger butter, fruit kompot served with dodgy dairy or scrumptious soya ice cream. Selection of soya ice creams neat £2.50. Various drinks 95p-£1.50.

Longsight

Misty's Vegetarian Cafe

Unit 3, Longsight Shopping Centre
531 Stockport Road, Longsight
Greater Manchester M12 4JH
Tel: 0161 256 3355 Fax:
Open: Mon-Wed & Sat 9-18.00, Thu-Fri 9-22.00, Sun 11-17.00

Vegetarian café with food from many cultures, virtually all of it vegan with an awesome range of vegan desserts. All day veggie breakfast £1.50-2.40 with all the usual plus chips, baked potatoes, toasted sandwiches. Starters £1-2 like pumpkin soup, carrot and coriander soup, Jamaican pattie. Salads £1.80-2.00 like felafel and salad in pitta, fried aubergine salad in pitta. Mains £2.50-3.00 such as aubergine and coconut curry with rice; veggie shepherd's pie; smoky tofu bake; American chilli and rice with avocado; Sunday nut roast vegan dinner with roast taties and veg plus pudding all for £4 at 1pm; stuffed peppers. Attention all other café owners! 10 out of the 11 desserts are vegan, £1-1.80, with a vast range of home baked vegan cakes, vegan cheesecakes, fruit crumble, sponge pudding, vegan ice cream. On Friday nights you can get a full 3 course meal for £5. Bring your own booze, no corkage charge. (Herb) teas 65p pot, 50p cup, coffee 60p, soya milk and milkshakes. If you don't like money, Manchester LETS scheme gives 25% discount payable in, er, bobbins. Also parties, weddings and meetings, cakes to order, and you can book the whole café on a closed night. One of the best vegan cafés ever.

Manchester

Cafe Pop

34-36 Oldham Street
Manchester, Greater Manchester M1 1JN
Tel: 0161 237 9688 Fax:
Open: Mon-Sat 9.30-17.30. Sun 10.30-16.30 at certain times of the year.

Vegetarian café with cosmoplitan cuisine. Selection of hot snacks like sauté mushrooms, thick toasties, crunchy Zorba salad. Wide selection of combination salads such as aubergine, tabouleh, Italian (griddled courgettes, tomatoes, peppers, onions, dressing). 3 or 4 main course specials daily from around the world - Chinese, Indian, Italian, Greek etc. Cakes, sometimes apple crumble, pumpkin pie. Tea 80p, coffee 95p, soya milk. 10% discount for Vegetarian and Vegan Society.

Frog & Bucket Comedy Club

111 Newton Street
Manchester
Tel: 0161 236 9805 Fax:
Doors open 19.30, show 21.00-23.30. Closed Tue-Wed.
Vegetarian comedy club. Main show Thu-Sat. Mon is raw
night, for up and coming comedians, hosted by an established
compere. Alternate Sundays there's the Comedy Express
improvisation group, like the TV show Whose Line Is It
Anyway? £6 on the door. Food features chilli, curry and rice,
hummus, salad.

Kallisti Café

at New Aeon Books
110 Tib Street, Manchester M4 1LR
Tel: 0161 839 9293 Fax: 0161 834 4493
Open: Mon-Sat 10-18.30, Sun 12-16.30
Vegetarian snack bar and bookshop-café with 21 seats. No
salads or starters but 3 vegan and 6 veggie main dishes 80p-
£1.45 such as corn and chilli burrito, bean quesadilia. 8 vegan
and 5 veggie sweets 45-90p like flapjacks and Green & Black's
vegan chocolate. Teas or coffee 60p, soya milk. Approx 10%
discount to VSUK, Vegan Soc, Viva!, PeTA, Animal Aid, varies
on item.

On the Eighth Day

107-111 Oxford Road
Manchester M1 7DU
Tel: 0161 2731850/4878 Fax: 0161-273 4878
Open: Mon-Fri 9-19.00, Sat 9-16.30
Big vegetarian café, take-away and shop in the middle of Manc
run by a cooperative with a top menu of great value grub, plenty of it vegan. Start with vegan pate and bread or vegan soup
£1.20-1.55. Also breads, jacket spuds, Indian snacks, roast
veg. Salads £1.75-2.95 such as vegan potato salad in mayo-
style dressing or coleslaw, a variety of fresh vegetable, bean,
rice and pasta salads. Main course specials with a crisp green

salad £2.95, with always some sort of vegan casserole or stew type dish, e.g. Caribbean with sweet potato, coconut, chilli and peanut sauce. Also a daily baked dish, for example pasta Arabbiatta. They also have a range of specials prepared to order, including Mediterranean style vegetables roasted in olive oil and herbs and served with hot ciabatta or brown rice. Vegan chocolate cake, steamed sponge pudding with soya custard or passion cake £1.25-1.50. Teas 75p, coffee 85p, vegan cappuccino £1-1.20. Bring your own booze, no corkage charge. Also full monty veggie breakfast till 11.30 £2.95, or something lighter like beans on toast £1.20.

Shop open Mon-Sat 9.30-17.30 with a wide range of vegetarian and vegan foods, wines, herbal supplements, cosmetics and fancy goods.

Outside catering service.

Rusholme

Punjab Sweet House

177 Wilmslow Road
Rusholme
Greater Manchester M14
Tel: 0161 225 2960 Fax:
Open every day 12-23.00, Fri-Sat till 24.00
Indian vegetarian restaurant with quite a lot of vegan food.

The Greenhouse

331 Great Western Street
Rusholme, Greater Manchester M14 4AN
Tel: 0161 224 0730 Fax: 0161 256 0943
Open: Mon-Sat 12-24.00, Sun 12-23.30, Xmas day 19.00
The original vegetarian restaurant in Manchester since 1983 with 100 a la carte dishes, half of them vegan. A stunning 30 desserts, of which just under half are vegan. With such an amazing choice, we'll just list some of the vegan delights and hope the book's big enough. 'Ere we go. Starters £1.85-2.95 include soup of the day with toasted granary roll; vegan garlic baguette; vegan gazpacho spicy Mexican soup served cold with organic taco chips; vegan oyster mushrooms in red wine marinade; falafel; pasta; hazelnut paté; veg samosas; spring roll; hummous and pitta; mezze. Main courses £4.95-6.95

such as Szechuan style egg plant with okra, oyster mushrooms and other veg cooked with fresh ginger and garlic in a dark Chinese sauce, served with a traditional Chinese, pineapple and cashew nut rice and a side salad; chilli bean and taco shells with gazpacho and organic tortilla chips; luxury cashew nut roast and red wine sauce enriched with soya cream; cashew pilau stuffed capsicums; hazelnut roast and apple gravy; vegan haggis; tamarind chilli; vegetable masala; specials of the day. Daytime specials from noon-17.00 are £2.95-4.95 such as Spanish chick peas; rice-stuffed vine leaves; saag aloo; hot avocado n' garlic 'naise; broccoli & Scheese fillo parcel; burrito with salsa sauce. Full monty Sunday roast £9.45, a rich and moist layered roast with a dark outer layer of cashew nut and walnut, a contrasting layer of almond and lemon around a core of mushroom and cashew nut paté, served with wild mushrooms, madeira sauce, roast potatoes, parsnips and fresh veg, cranberry and apple sauces and a side salad. Lots of afternoon cake. And now for the awesomest of awesome dessert menus £1.95-2.65 including a choice of vegan ice creams; apple strudel; fruit crumble; fresh fruit salad; carrot and sultana cake; banana and walnut cake; apricot and almond cake; chocolate cake; daily specials. Good selection of spirits, wines and beers including organic. Kids welcome. 10% discount for Vegetarian or Vegan Society and students (except Sat after 17.00, Xmas, New Year and Valentine's).

West Didsbury

Greens Restaurant

43 Lapwing Lane, West Didsbury
Greater Manchester M20 2NT
Tel: 0161-434 4259 Fax: 0161-448 0120
Open: Every day 17.50-22.30, also Tue-Fri 12-14.00.
Fantastic modern international and ethnic vegetarian restaurant. 4 veggie and 4 vegan entrées £2.50-4.75 like norimaki sushi rolls of roasted seaweed wrapped around sticky rice and vegetables, served with hot wasabi horseraddish. 2 veggie and 2 vegan salads £5 such as Panzanella roasted Mediterranean vegetables with fresh chilli and red wine soaked ciabatta croutons. 3 vegan and 4 veggie main courses include golden sweet potato fried with red onion, chilli, mango and okra served

between slices of griddled pineapple, topped with coconut spiced sauce. 5 desserts £3.50 include dairy-free chocolate cake. Coffee £1. Bring your own booze, no corkage charge.

Withington

60/40 Café

448 Wilmslow Road, Withington
Greater Manchester M20 3BW
Tel: 0161 295 1525 Fax:
Open every day 10.00-00.30
Vegetarian restaurant with very varied menu including Indian and Mexican, though vegans may be disappointed at the high amounts of cheese and total lack of vegan desserts. Start with dips and nibbles, soup, garlic mushrooms or continental deep fried vegetables in herb batter £1.20-3.00. 3 vegan and 4 veggie salads £4 such as Caesar or Greek. 2 vegan and several veggie main courses £5 like spinach lasagne; chimichangas, matar paneer, burritos, gnocchi, tacos. Jacket spuds £2, fillings 45-75p. Sticky toffee pudding, summer fruit crumble or home made cake and filter coffee £2.50, but none of them vegan alas. Sandwiches £2.25-2.50 with baguette, pitta, brown or white bread including vegan humus and salad. Three course evening mean from 6pm for £8.50.

LANCASHIRE

Blackpool

Wildlife Hotel

39 Woodfield Road, Blackpool
Lancashire FY1 6AX
Tel: 01253 346143 Fax:
3 single £16-£20, 4 double and 4 twin, all en suite.
The owners are vegan at this fully licensed, exclusively vege-tarian hotel just off Blackpool Promenade. Tea/coffee, tv in all rooms, also breakfast in rooms available. Veg or vegan break-fasts of course, as well as gluten free diets catered for and an

evening meal for only £5, great value. Bar and TV lounge. Close to pleasure beach and those wonderful trams. Recommended by politicians and charity representatives who use Wildlife when doing some lobbying at the conferences - keep up the good work. Between central and south piers. Discount for VSUK & Vegan Soc., Animal Aid, PETA and Viva! members.

The Invernia Guest House

10 Kirby Road, Blackpool
Lancashire FY1 6EB
Tel: 01253 21636
2 single £10-£15, 5 double £20-£30, 4 family £25-38
Open: Easter to November and some winter weekends.
Omnivorous guest house run by vegetarians, so the options are available. Tea/coffee and tv in rooms. Bar and tv lounge.

Evening meal £4. Situated close to the promenade and central for all attractions. Leave promenade at Manchester Hotel, then first left after green man crossing.

Bolton

Patagonia Cafe

129 Bradshawgate
Bolton, Lancashire BL2 1BJ
Tel: 01204 528 533 Fax: 01204 528533
Mon-Sat 9.00-17.00 closed Sunday.
Omnivorous café that considers itself a crossover for mixed families with members from all camps, and it does have a large proportion of veggie choices. Also it's the only American style coffee house in Bolton, for all those *Frasier and Friends* fans. Toast, cereal and bagels 55p-£1.45. Soup and quiche. Salad bowl £2.50-£2.75. Baked potatoes £1.95. Various cakes and ice creams.

Burnley

Red Triangle Cafe

160 St James Street
Burnley, Lancashire BB11 1NR
Tel: 01282 832 319 Fax:
Tues-Sat 10.30-19.00, Fri & Sat night 19.30-22.30
Closed Sun & Mon
Veggie café and restaurant that also has monthly music nights. Starters such as garlic mushrooms or soup £1.50. Mains include stuffed butternut squash, tagliatelle, or risotto for £2.80 during the day or £5 at night. Selection of salads. Desserts £1.50. Wine only £4.95 a bottle.

Clitheroe

The Jigsaw Pantry

Trinity Youth & Comunity Centre, Weslyan Row
Clitheroe, Lancashire BB7 2JY. Tel: 01200 27886.
Open Mon-Wed 12-13.15. Closed last Wed of month.
This vegetarian wholefood café and takeaway is part of a dis-

ability training rights and employment organization. Seasonal homemade menu with soup from 75p. Mushroom strudel or Provençal tartlets £2.10. Vegan and vegetarian sandwiches £1.25 to takeaway.

Lancaster

Libra

19 Brock Street
Lancaster LA1 1UR
Tel: 01524 61551 Fax:
Open: Mon-Sat 9-16.30, closed Sun
Vegetarian café which caters well for vegans.

The Whale Tail

78a Penny Street
Lancaster LA1 1XN
Tel: 01524 845 133 Fax:
Mon-Fri 9.00-17.00, Sat 9.00-18.00, Sun 10.30-15.30
Vegetarian café offering starters such as spiced potatoes, sweet corn chowder, paté £1.60-£2.25. Various salads, 6 mains at £3.95. Vegan sticky toffee pudding, banoffee pie, banana & chocolate cake £1.50-£1.95. House wine £5.95.

Oldham

Woody's

5 King Street, Delph
Saddleworth, Oldham
Lancashire OL3 5DL
Tel: 01457 871 197 Fax: 0161 678 8389
Thur, Fri, Sat 19.30-23.00 only.
Vegetarian restaurant with large vegan and gluten free selection. Starters £2.65-£3.25 such as oriental parcel, leek tartlet, avocado salsa etc. Mains £7.95-£8.95 include terrine, carnival slice, okra & bean parcel, nut loaf, crêpes, cider choux buns, all with veg of the day. Wine from £7.75.

Pendle

Jim's Caff
19-21 New Market Street
Pendle, Lancashire BB8 9BJ
Tel: 01282 868 828 Fax:
Open: Thu-Sun 19-23.00
Licensed vegetarian restaurant with some vegan food.

Tolmorden

Bear Cafe
29 Rochdale Road
Todmorden
Lancashire OL14 7LA
Tel: 01706 819 690 Fax:
Open: Mon-Sat 9.30-17.00, closed Sun
Vegetarian café with some vegan food.

MERSEYSIDE

Heswall

Crispins Restaurant
106 Telegraph Road
Heswall, Merseyside L60 0AQ
Tel: 0151 342 8750 Fax:
Everyday 12.00-14.00 & 18.30-22.00
Omnivorous restaurant with at least 4 starters and 4 mains that are vegetarian.

Green Fish Café

11 Upper Newington
Liverpool, Merseyside L1
Tel: 0151 707 0764 Fax:
Mon-Sat 11.00-18.00. Closed Sun.
Vegetarian café. Entrées £1.30-1.50 include soup, hummus
etc. 3 vegan and 1 veggie salads change daily and are 75p for
one, £1.50 for a mix. One vegan and 5 veggie main courses
£2.75-3.50 such as vegetable lasagne, mousakka, spinach
curry, Mexican burritos, pizza, bakes, pasta etc. Desserts 80p-
£1 include carrot cake, fruit pies, flan, apple tray bake, scones.
Teas 70p, coffee 60p. No soya milk.

The Egg Cafe

Newington Buildings
16-18 Newington (Top Floor)
Liverpool, Merseyside L1 4ED
Tel: 0151-707 2755 Fax:
Open Mon-Sat 09.00-23.00. Sun 10.00-18.30.
Eclectic vegetarian café. Most food is vegan and the menu
changes daily. Starters include garlic bread £1.40, soup and
garlic bread £2.25. Salads £1.10-2.00 e.g. pasta salad with
peanuts and herbs; beetroot and apricot. Vegan main courses
include potato and aubergine sweet curry with rice £4.75;
shepherd's pie & salad £3.95; spicy burger with relish, pitta
and salad £2.90; chillie and rice £3.95. Also lasagna and
salad £3.95; aubergine Daube and rice £4.75. Vegan spicy
apple crumble £1.65, lemon torte £1.75, chocolate fudge cake
£1.50. Teas 80p, coffee 85p, soya milk available and soya milkshakes. Some half portions available. £1 corkage. No non-
smoking area. 50 seats. Highchairs available.

Greenbank Restaurant

332-338 Smithdown Road
Liverpool
Merseyside L15 3AM
Tel: 0151 734 4498 Fax:
11.00-23.00 all week, till 22.30 Sunday.
Large vegetarian option.

GOING ON HOLIDAY ABROAD?

Check out the overseas vegetarian guides
at the end of this book.

ORDER THIS BOOK FOR A FRIEND

See our order form on page 251

Vegetarian Guides Ltd, the world's leading
publisher for the world's most
discerning diners.

UNCAGED

CAMPAIGNS TO END VIVISECTION

Uncaged Campaigns is one of the most active and dynamic anti-vivisection organisation in the UK. Our outlook is positive and democratic; we are committed to achieving the abolition of vivisection by working with a wide range of sympathetic organisations and turning public concern for animals into concrete political action.

We are working hard to achieve our goal of ending vivisection. In our brief history we have already reached millions of people with our positive campaign against animal experiments.

WE DON'T GIVE UP

Rage Against The Cage (saturday june 6th 1998)
Every year Uncaged organises the national march against vivisection. The event attracts thousands of people and captures the attention of the media and the public. 'Rage' has grown in size each year and is now an exciting carnival style event with music, food, stalls, speakers, fun and a really positive atmosphere with a hard hitting message.

Global Boycott Of Procter & Gamble
Our longest running campaign is the building of a consumer boycott against P&G. This is now a worldwide campaign. The international pressure on P&G to stop testing on animals is growing - other companies have changed their policies under this kind of consumer pressure.

Pigs Might Fly
Plundering pigs organs to use as spare parts for humans would be both cruel and highly dangerous. The evidence of virus transferral has led the Government to place a moratorium on clinical trials: we aim to turn this into a permanent ban. The tide of public opinion is turning in our favour - this is one battle we can win.

Uncaged Campaigns' sister organisation - **Uncaged Educational Trust** - (registered charity no. 1041426) was founded in 1994. The trust was created to present to educators, school children and the public, the human and non-human cost of vivisection, and to promote effective and humane scientific research.

JOIN UNCAGED CAMPAIGNS

Uncaged Campaigns relies on your support to help stop vivisection.

**Uncaged Campaigns
14 Ridgeway Road
Sheffield
S12 2SS
Tel: (0114) 253 0020
Fax: (0114) 265 4070
E-mail: uncaged.anti-viv@dial.pipex.com
Website: http://www.uncaged.co.uk**

1. Uncaged Campaigns takes the global day of action onto Procter & Gamble's doorstep in Newcastle **2.** A stunt using a restraining device attracts media attention to our cause **3.** Rage Against The Cage 1997 **4.** Benjamin Zephaniah lends his support to our campaign **5.** Willow & Eddie rescued from vivisection by Uncaged Campaigns.

NORTH EAST

CLEVELAND

Eaglescliffe

The Waiting Room

9 Station Road, Eaglescliffe, Cleveland TS16 0BU
Tel: 01642 780 465
Mon-Sat 11.00-14.30 & 19.00-22.00. Sun 10-14.30, 19-21.30.
Vegetarian. Lunchtime menu offers soup £1.60, paté with cru-
dités, sandwiches £1.25, salads and ploughman's. Also main
courses from a similar menu to the dinner one. Speaking of
which, starters such as melon & sorbet, Indian savouries, potatoe wedges, paté £2-£3.05. Mains from the selection on a
blackboard are priced by size. Small one dish £6.60; medium
selection of two £6.95; and large three or more dishes £7.30.
Mains include carrot & mushroom loaf, moussaka, stroganoff,
curry, pasta, crustade, croquettes, stuffed peppers, casserole,
pie, haloumi etc. Desserts £2.85-3.05 such as sorbet, sticky
toffee, banoffee, choc cheesecake. House wine £7.05, or bring
your own for £2 corkage. They suggest ringing first, if vegan,
to check that day's menu.

Stockton on Tees

The Food Parcel

Stockton International Family Center
66 Dovecot Street, Stockton on Tees
Cleveland. Tel: 01642 612400 Fax: 01642 608432
Open: Mon-Fri 12.15-13.30
Vegetarian café and takeaway. 20 starters from 75p with inter-
esting soups including borsht, pakoras, falafel, daal. (OK
Steve?) 30 salads and 30 main courses £2-£2.50 such as stir
fry veg, chickpea Wellington, dansak, pancakes, pizza,
lasagne, lentil flan. Desserts 50-65p. Tea 25p and coffee 30p.
Great value.

COUNTY DURHAM

Barnard Castle

Kirkorah

11 Galgate, Barnard Castle
County Durham DL12 8EQ
Tel: 01833-637 146 Fax:
Open: summer every day 08.30-22.00
New 75% vegetarian restaurant with one or two vegan dishes daily, open for breakfast, lunch and dinner. The cook is Vegetarian Society Cordon Vert trained. Tea garden at the back. Also a shop with bric-a-brac and secondhand clothes.

Darlington

Bakehouse Hill Restaurant

3-5 Bakehouse Hill, Market Square
Darlington, County Durham
Tel: 01325 481 931 Fax:
Mon-Sat 9-16.30
Coffee shop with heaps of veggie food.

Durham

Molly's Wholefood Store & Cafe

5 North Terrace, Framwellgate Moor
Durham, County Durham DH1 5EF
Tel: 0191 386 2216 Fax:
Mon-Fri 9.00-18.00 Sat till 17.00 closed Sun
Vegetarian café offering sarnies 99p-£1.30, baked spuds + fillings 70p-£1.10, salads and soups. Range of pasties, quiches, Mexican savouries etc 90p-£1.50. Loads of cakes, scones, biscuits, slices and fruit. Various teas, coffees, non caffeines and even some beer. Everything possible is organic and fair traded.

HUMBERSIDE

Hull

Hitchcocks

1 Bishops Lane, Hull
Tel: 01482 320 233
Open: 20.15 till late.
Open when bookings made, first person to book decides cuisine for evening. It may be vegetarian, Italian, Mexican, Afro Caribbean, Greek.Thai or whatever. Buffet style with three courses for £10 (£8 concessions). Popular with local students. Fun and funky which is not suprising with wine at £5 a bottle.

The Zoo Café

80B Newland Avenue
Hull, Humberside HU5 3BA
Tel: 01482 494 352 Fax:
Mon-Sat 10.00-18.00 closed Sunday.
Vegetarian café offering selections from a daily changing menu. Veggie burgers are the only thing always available. Choose from soup, salads, burritos, casseroles. Also brownies, flapjack, treacle tart etc. Mainly vegan.

NORTH YORKSHIRE

Giggleswick

Woodlands Country House Hotel

Woodlands, The Mains
Giggleswick, North Yorkshire
Tel: 01729 822058 Fax:
Omnivorous guest house with 1 single £16 & 1 en suite £18; 1 double & 2 en suite £28-£36; 1 twin & 1 en suite £28-£36; 1 family £36-£42. TV, tea/coffee in rooms. Bar and TV lounge. Offers veg or vegan option for breakfast and dinner for £8-£10. Situated in beautiful North Yorkshire with its scenic delights.

Swinstey Tea Gardens

Fewston House, Fewston
Harrogate, North Yorkshire HG3 1SU
Tel: 01943 880637 Fax: 01943 880637
Open Sat & Sun 11-17.00

Vegetarian café with French, Indian, Italian, Mediterranean, Balkan and wholefood cuisine. Mixed vegetable vegan soup £2.70, mixed salad, 1 vegetarian and 1 vegan main course £3.95-4.75 e.g. stuffed peppers with oven baked vegetables in olive oil; chick pea Wellington with peppers, tomatoes and fresh basil sauce. Choice of organic, gluten free, vegan and fat free cakes. Teas 95p, coffee £1. Soya milk available.

Wild Ginger Vegetarian Café Bistro

5 Station Parade
Harrogate, North Yorkshire HG4 3LG
Tel: 01423 566122 Fax:
Mon-Sat 10.00-16.00 closed Sundays.

Organic vegan menu, though apparently they keep some cow juice 'under the counter'. Starters include pitta & salad with dips, hoummous, guacamole, soup etc. £1.95-£2.45. Selection of salads. Mains £3.95-£6.25, choose from butterbean roast, stuffed marrow, hot pot, mushroom pie, risotto etc. Desserts include pineapple upside down pudding, fruit crumble, chocolate cake, carrot cake, ice cream £1.20-£2.50. Selection of organic beers and wines.

Amadeus Vegetarian Hotel

115 Franklin Road
Harrowgate, North Yorkshire HG1 5EN
Tel: 01423-505151 Fax: 01423-505151

Vegetarian hotel. Open all year excluding Xmas. 1 single room £26-30; 1 double en suite (bath) £50-60; 2 twin en suite (shower) £46-56. Tea/coffee and TV in rooms. Lounge. Both proprietors are vegetarian. Veggie and vegan breakfasts available with veggie sausages, muesli, soya milk & vegan marg. Evening meal £15.

10 mins walk north from town centre and railway station. Half mile to veggie cafe, 10 mins walk to Turkish baths, 40 mins drive to Yorkshire Dales and York.

Hawes

Tea Tree

Outhwaite House, Main Street, Hawes
North Yorkshire DL8 3QW
Tel: 01969 667 817
Tue-Sun 11.00-17.00. Closed Mon.
Vegetarian café with crumpets, scones, tea cakes and a cream tea for £2.50. Also various things on toast £2-£2.25, sandwiches and stuffed pitta £1.85-£2.75. Soup of the day, bean salad, baked potatoes and ploughman's with pickles.

Ingleton

Prospect Cottage

Bank End, Ingleton
North Yorkshire LA6 3HE
Tel: 015242 41328 Fax:
1 single £14.50-£16, 1 double £29-£32
Vegetarian b&b in picturesque stone built house situated within the old village of Ingleton, overlooking the river Greta valley. No tv so you'll have to actually talk to your partner or other folk. Tea/coffee in rooms and radio. The village has shops, bakeries, bank and a post office, plus cafés and pubs where a veggie option can can be found. In the Yorkshire Dales and on the doorstep of the Lake District. Caves, waterfalls, potholes and mountains nearby. Discount for VSUK, Vegan Society, Animal Aid, PETA, Viva!, Uncaged and Green Party members. Directions: Pick up from railway, 11 miles north of Settle and 17 miles south of Kendal. Ingleton is just off A65, past Bridge Hotel and up main street for 300 yards, then Prospect Cottage is on left.

Scarborough

The Ranworth Vegetarian Guesthouse

Ranworth, Church Rd
Ravenscar, Scarborough
North Yorkshire YO13 OLZ
Tel: 01723 870366 Fax:
3 double & 1 twin £17

Stone built Victorian former vicarage with large gardens over-looking the village cricket pitch, offering vegetarian wholefood catering. All rooms have space for a cot, also highchair provided. Plus a playroom filled with books and toys for children, though I'm sure if you ask nicely they will let you have a go with the train set. Veg or vegan dinner £8. Walking starts right at the front door, there's a beach nearby, a pool in the village and a pub. Aromatherapy massage available. From A171 Scarborough-Whitby Road take turning marked Ravenscar 5 miles.

Flower In Hand Guest House

Burr Bank, Scarborough, North Yorkshire YO11 1PN
Tel: 01723 371471 Fax: 01723 507800
b.hampshire@which.net
Open all year.

Omnivorous bed and breakfast. Set in quiet cul-de-sac with superb sea views yet close to the town centre, beach, and all attractions. 3 doubles en suite £17.50 per person; 1 family room £17.50 per person; half price for children sharing. Tea/coffee, washbasins, and TV in rooms. Veggie and vegan breakfasts available including muesli, soymilk & vegan marg. Information on local veggie dining freely available.
Directions: From South Beach head north on Foreshore Road, turning left (away from Ocean) on small side road between Newcastle Packet Pub and Princess Cafe. 200 yards up steep hill.

Settle

Sansbury Place Vegetarian Guesthouse

Duke Street, Settle, North Yorkshire BD24 9AS
Tel: 01729 823840 Fax:
1 single £19-£22, 2 double £38-£44
Open all year except last 3 weeks of Jan.
Spacious Victorian house with a secluded garden and splendid
views of the surrounding hills. Children 5 and over welcome.
Open fire in guest sitting room. Dinner is veg. or vegan using
organic wholefoods £12. Local attractions are Settle to Carlisle
railway, Swaledale, Wensleydale, Wharfedale, Ingleton Falls,
Malham Cove etc. 10% discount to VSUK and Vegan Society
Members. Few minutes walk from Settle station. Or follow
signs from A65 Settle bypass.

Skipton

Herbs Restaurant

10 High Street, Skipton, North Yorkshire BD23 1JZ
Tel: 01756 790 619
Mon & Wed-Sat 9.30-16.45 closed Sun & Tues.
Vegetarian wholefood restaurant and take away in natural food
centre. Soup and pate £1.75. Salads, savouries include filled
pancakes, flans, bakes, burgers, crumble from £3.25-£4.35.
Desserts include carrot cake, bilberry & almond tart, sticky
prune cake, apple & mincemeat 45p-£1.75.

Whitby

Ryedale House

154-8 Coach Road, Sleights, Nr Whitby
North Yorkshire YO22 5EQ
Tel: 01947 810534. Open Mar-Oct.
2 double en-suite £17.50-£19, 1 twin en-suite £17.50-£18.50
Veggie breakfast available in charming cottage style home at
the foot of the moors, in the Esk valley with panoramic views.
Sun terrace and landscaped garden, also plants for sale. Good
local walking, quiet countryside except by the local steam railway, nearby coast etc. On A169 Pickering-Whitby road, 250
metres from Plough Inn.

SHEPHERD'S PURSE

Whitby

BED & BREAKFAST

Vegetarian Restaurant

Wholefoods

Dress Shop

Galleried courtyard of en-suite rooms.

Four-poster or brass bedsteads and country furniture.

95 CHURCH STREET · WHITBY
YO22 4BH · Tel : (01947) 820228

Falcon Guest House

29 Falcon Terrace, Whitby
North Yorkshire YO21 1EH
Tel: 01947 603507 Fax:
2 family rooms £15

Vegetarian b&b in a small friendly guesthouse in a quiet location just 7 minutes walk from the town and harbour. No evening meal available. All the delights of Whitby on offer and the wonderful North Yorkshire Moors.

Directions: take Windsor Terrace, the road between the bus and rail stations, up the hill then last road on right.

Shepherd's Purse

95 Church Street
Whitby, North Yorkshire YO22 4BH
Tel: 01947 820228

Vegetarian bed and breakfast with 9 rooms, five of them en suite, offering well appointed and comfortable accommodation in a friendly atmosphere. Some rooms galleried and overlooking the courtyard and garden. Wholefood restaurant and wholefood shop on the premises, in the heart of the lovely old town.

Wentworth House

27 Hudson Street, West Cliff
Whitby, North Yorkshire YO21 3EP
Tel: 01947 602433 Fax:
1 single £17, 3 double en suite £19, 2 twin en suite £19 and 1
family room.

Four storey Victorian house run by veggies offering spacious accommodation just 5 minutes walk from the town centre.
Tea/coffee and radio alarms in rooms. Beautiful coastline and countryside, historic town and harbour (watch out for Dracula).
Follow signs to town centre, straight over roundabout at station towrds harbour, don`t cross bridge, carry along harbourside

towards pier, just before pier turn left up cliff. At junction take left then straight over next crossroad and is halfway along road on left hand side. About 2 mins. From harbour.

York

Vegetarian B&B

21 Park Grove
York, North Yorkshire YO3 7LG
Tel: 01904 644790 Fax:
Open all year.
Exclusively vegetarian bed and breakfast accommodation in a spacious Victorian town house in a quiet locality only ten minutes walk from the centre of York and the Minster.   One single £18; one double with toilet, bath & shower £36; one twin with toilet, bath & shower £36. Tea and coffee making and a clock radio in each room. Substantial breakfasts including soya marg, soya milk, soysausages, and vegan muesli. TV lounge. No evening meal available, but there are vegetarian restaurants in York. Non-smoking. Residents' parking. Note that there is no B&B sign outside.

Dairy Guest House

3 Scarcroft Road, York
North Yorkshire YO2 1ND
Tel: 01904 639367 Fax:
February to December.
1 single £28 & 1 en suite £38, 1 double £18 & 1 en suite £22.50, 1 twin £18 & 1 en suite £22.50, 1 family £18.
Vegetarian run Victorian town house, set around a flower filled courtyard offers accommodation in charming cottage styled rooms. Veggie breakfast available. Close to the city centre with all York has to offer, the Minster, museums shopping, nightlife and days out to the wonderful countryside.

The Blake Head

104 Micklegate
York, North Yorkshire YO1 1JX
Tel: 01904 623 767 Fax:
9.30-17.00 everyday.
Vegetarian with hot lunches and loads of cakes and buns all day.

The Rubicon

5 Little Stonegate
York, North Yorkshire YO1 2AX
Tel: 01904 676 076 Fax:
Tues-Sat 12.00-14.00, Mon-Sun evenings 17.00-22.00
Vegetarian restaurant. 3 course dinner £12.50, 2 course £10. Starter selection includes Jamaican rissoles, butterbean pate, mushroom bake, hummous etc. Mains moussaka, tagine, tian, lasagne, stuffed pancakes. Choice of desserts crumble, fool, sticky toffee, trifle, bread & butter pudding. Gluten free options. Also daily specials. Unlicensed.

NORTHUMBERLAND

Berwick upon Tweed

Meadow House

The Village Green
East Ord, Berwick-upon-Tweed
Northumberland TD15 2NS
Tel: 01289 330679 Fax:
April 1st-Oct 31st. 1 double & 1 twin both en-suite £23-£28
Omnivorous B&B with vegetarian owners who are able to cater for vegans with advance notice. TV, tea/coffee, toiletries, bathrobe, hairdryer and local biscuits in rooms. Huge garden with croquet lawn and two summer houses. In a peaceful village on the green, 2 miles from Berwick and the Northumberland coast with Holy Island (Lindisfarne), St Abbs

Head, Farne Islands and miles of sandy beaches. Won B&B of the year from ETB in 1996.
Directions: East Ord is just off A1 Newcastle-Edinburgh Road.

SOUTH YORKSHIRE

Bradford

Ivy Guest House

3 Melbourne Place
Bradford, South Yorkshire BD5 0HZ
Tel: 01274 727060 Fax:
2 single £18, 5 twin & 5 double £30
Breakfast only, 10% discount for Vegetarian and Vegan Society members.

Doncaster

Wholefoods

Copley Road, Doncaster
South Yorkshire
Tel: 01302 738 730 Fax:
Open: Mon-Sat 9-17.00, closed Sun.
Also Thu-Sat 19.30-22.30.
Vegetarian restaurant with vegan food.

Sheffield

Blue Moon Café

220 Norfolk Row, Sheffield
South Yorkshire
Tel: 0114 2763443 Fax:
Mon-Sat 8.00-16.30
Vegetarian in an informal self service setting with blackboard menu. Breakfast till 11.00 croissant or cereal 80p, toast 35p, scrambled eggs £1.80. Main meals are changed and at least one is vegan, 6 salads, soup £1.80, pizza, hommity, jamaican patties. Variety of cakes most of which are vegan, tea, coffee and juices.

TYNE & WEAR

Newcastle

Bob Trollop

32-40 Sandhill, Quayside
Newcastle, Tyne & Wear NE1 3JF
Tel: 0191 261 1037 Fax:
Open: Mon-Sat 11-23.00, Sun 12-22.30

100% Vegetarian PUB with a full menu available 11-19.00 Mon-Sat and 10-19.00 Sun. This is such a fine idea we've listed almost the entire menu to inspire everyone to go there, help them make loads of dosh and expand to take over every pub in the land. Starters 99p-£1.95 like garlic bread, samosas, mushroom pate with toast, pakoras, tacos. Dips with salad garnish £2.45-3.65: deep fried coated veg with peanut satay sauce; jacket wedges with garlic mayonnaise; vegetable nuggets with tomato and garlic dip; tikka trianges; extra dips 55p. Jacket spuds £1.65-2.65 with loads of fillings. All day breakfast £2.75. Mixed grill £3.25 with veggie sausages, one diet burger, spicy beanburger, tomato, garlic mushrooms, onion rings and jacket wedges. Main courses! Tagliatelle Nicoise £3.95 or vegetable lasange £3.75, both with salad and jacket potato. Specials £2.65-3.45 bean hot top, veggie chilli, Stroganoff, vegetable casserole; in pancakes, with hash browns, wholegrain rice, or jacket wedges. Giant Yorkshire pudding filled with veggie sausages, onions, mashed potato and vegetarian gravy £3.40. Hot butties, a wholemeal roll or bagel with either veggie sausages, a spicy beanburger, a quarterpounder (all £1.45) or a half pounder £2.25. And not a McClown in sight. Filled bagels or wholemeal rolls £1.25. And finally the desserts £1.75-1.95 include apricot or apple crumble, chocolate fudge cake, cherry pancake, treacle sponge and pina colada gateaux; vegan status of these is unknown. Various coffes and teas 50-80p. Happy hour 4-7pm. with cut price wine, draught beers, lager and cider.

Red Herring Workers Co-operative

3/4 Studley Terrace, Nunns Moor Road
Newcastle Upon Tyne, Tyne & Wear NE4 5AH
Tel: 0191 272 3484 Fax:
Open Tue-Sat 10am-late. Closed Sun & Mon.
Wholefood vegetarian cafe and restaurant which is 50%
vegan. Main courses served 10am-9.45pm. Cold snacks to
take away; plus freshly baked bread and cakes sold 9.30-
5.00pm. 8+ entrees £1.60-2.75 e.g. red pepper dip, Patlican
Tava. 3 salads £1.25-2.50 e.g. Chilean, Gujarati. 4-6 main
courses £2.20-6.95 e.g. curried pastie, Winter Veggie Hotpot,
quiche, burgers, pizza. Menu changes daily. 4-6 mostly vegan
desserts £2.20-2.75 e.g. fruit crumble cheesecake, banana
split. Bring your own alcohol, free corkage. Non-smoking area.
Highchairs and children's portions. Wheelchair

The Supernatural Restaurant

2 Upper Level, Princess Square
Newcastle, Tyne & Wear NE1 8ER
Tel: 0191 261 2730 Fax:
Open: Tue-Fri 10.30-19.30. Mon,Sat 10.30-19.00. Sun closed.
Vegetarian restaurant with Chinese, Indian, Italian,
Mediterranean and Mexican food such as lentil and veg curry,
Moroccan couscous, spinach pasta. 5 vegan and 8 veggie
starters £1.65-3.75. 5 vegan and 9 veggie salads £2.30. 4
vegan and 6 veggie main courses £2.95-3.75. 1 vegan and 4
veggie desserts £1.05-1.25. Beer, wine £1.15 glass, teas 65p,
coffee 60p, soya milk. Student discount 10%.

Heartbreak Soup

77 Quayside, Newcastle
Tyne & Wear
Tel: 0191 222 1701 Fax:
Mon-Sat 12.00-15.00 & 19.00-22.00 closed Sunday
Lively international Tex-Mex restaurant with big selection of
veggie alternatives.

WEST YORKSHIRE

Bradford

Hansa's Gujarati Vegetarian

44 Great Horton Road
Bradford, West Yorkshire BD7 1AL
Tel: 01274 736 008 Fax:
Mon-Thu 18.00-20.30, Fri & Sat 18.00-23.30, Sun 12.00-22.00
Indian vegetarian restaurant and take away, also second
branch in Leeds. Starters £2.25-£3.95 Mains £3.95-£5.95
biriyani, daal, curry variations etc. All the usual desserts £2.25-
£395. Discount for VSUK and Vegan Society members.

South Square Vegetarian Cafe

South Square, Thornton Road
Thornton, Bradford
West Yorkshire BD13 3LD
Tel: 01274 843928 Fax:
Open Tue-Sat 10.30-16.30, Sun 12-16.00. Mon closed.
Vegetarian cafe. Mix of fast food, Indian, Mediterranean and
Mexican dishes, with a wholefood approach. Entrees £1.80-
2.00 include: Lentil & tomato soup (vegan), carrot and corian-
der soup, green pea soup and lots more. Salads £2.00-2.40
include: potato salad, tomato and basil salad, and bean salad.
Main courses include canneloni, spicy chick pea casserole
(vegan) and pea and potato curry (vegan). Desserts £0.75-
1.40 include wholefood cakes, oat and orange cake (vegan).
Bring your own booze with free corkage. Tea 90p, coffee 80p.
Soya milk available. Wheelchair access. Highchairs for children. Non-smoking restaurant. 10% discount to members of
the Vegetarian and Vegan Society.

Halifax

Heatons Restaurant & Coffee House

11 Northgate, Halifax
West Yorkshire HX1 1UR
Mon-Sat 10.00-16.00 closed Sunday.
Vegetarian wholefood restaurant. Selection of toasted tea-cakes, scones and homemade cakes from 60p. Soup£1.75, salads, open sandwiches £2.75-£2.95, baked spuds, patties, pasta, casseroles etc.

Hedben Bridge

Hebden Lodge Hotel & V.B.'s Vegetarian Restaurant

6-10 New Road, Hebden Bridge
West Yorkshire HX7 8AD
Tel: 01422 845272 Fax:
15 rooms all en suite
3 crown vegetarian hotel, all rooms with the usual luxuries we like to enjoy. At the head of the beautiful Calder Valley with Bronte country seven miles away and the Peak District and Yorkshire Dales within easy reach, a lovely part of the world. V.B café bar and restaurant is open to non residents from 7.00-23.00 with an all day breakfast for £3.95, morning coffee or afternoon tea. Bistro menu at lunchtime has veggie burgers, pasties and pies £1.90-£2.95. Tapas at £2.25 or a selection for 2 people for £9.95. Pasta, casseroles, bakes and toad in the hole for around £4.50. Ice creams, lots of puddings. The gourmet dinner menu features 11 entrées with veg & fruit kebabs, bruchetta, corn fritters, pollenta etc £2.75-£4.25. Mains £5.95-£7.45 include asparagus loaf, torte, tortellini, risotto, gourgere, aubergine steaks et al. If you have room a selection of cakes, gateux, puddings, sweets and ice cream. Interesting and varied menu which is according to the Independent On Sunday "the most fantastic vegetarian restau-

rant in the universe." Lots of beers, wines and spirits.
Hebden Bridge is on the A646, from M62 westbound take exit
24 then A629 towards Halifax then follow A646 signs. From
M62 eastbound exit 21, follow signs for and then go past
Hollingsworth Lake, at T junction turn right on A58 towards
Halifax, then left on B6138 to Mytholmroyd, then left at T on to
A646 1 mile to Hebden Bridge.

Huddersfield

The Blue Rooms

9 Byam Arcade, Huddersfield
West Yorkshire HD1 1ND
Tel: 01484 512 373 Fax:
Mon-Sat 9.00-16.00
Vegetarian breakast, snacks, light lunch and buns.

Leeds

Bhavani Junction

2 Eastgate, Leeds
West Yorkshire LS2 7JL
Tel: 01532 468 988 Fax:
Mon-Sat 11.30-14.30 & 18.00-23.45 also Sun 11.30-14.30
Indian with separate veg menu and lunchtime buffet.

Hansa's Gujarati Vegetarian Restaurant

72-74 North Street
Leeds, West Yorkshire LS2 7PN
Tel: 01132 444 408 Fax:
Mon-Thur 18.00-20.30, Fri & Sat 18.00-21.30 closed Sun.
Same menu as Bradford Hansa`s.

Strawberry Fields Bistro

159 Woodhouse Lane
Leeds, West Yorkshire LS2 3ED
Tel: 0113 243 1515
Mon-Fri 11.45-14.00 & 18.00-20.30.
Sat 18.00-20.30. Closed Sun.
Omnivourous Italinate bistro in Leeds, offering a small selection of Mexican and pizza vegetarian choices.

Otley

The Curlew Cafe

11-13 Crossgate
Otley, West Yorkshire LS21 1AG
Tel: 01943 464 351 Fax:
Tue-Sat 11.00-15.00 & Fri-Sat 19.00-21.00, Sun 14.00-17.00.
Closed Mon
Vegetarain café. Starters £2-£3 with interesting soups, nachos, paté etc. Mains £3.95 during day and £6.95 in evenings include lentil bake, provencale stew, stroganof, cannelloni, mushroom loaf. Desserts from £1 in day and £2.20 evenings, choose from cakes, scones, crumbles, sticky toffee pud. Unlicensed so bring your own.

CUMBRIA - LAKELAND

Ambleside

Yewfield Vegetarian Guesthouse & Apartments

Hawkshead Hill
Hawkshead, Ambleside
Cumbria LA22 0PR
Tel: 015394 36765 Fax: 015394 36096
Two doubles and one twin all en suite £20-£28.50 per person.
Closed Mid Nov-Jan.

A high standard of accommodation is offered at this peaceful and quiet retreat in an elevated position, set in 25 acres of private grounds with panoramic views over lake Windermere and the fells. The rooms have satellite t/v, radio, tea/coffee and a lounge as well as a library area, very country house. Veggie breakfast though no evening meal, not a problem with the choice available in Lakeland (see other listings). Also 4 self catering apartments, 3 sleep 2 and the other 4, in the former coach house & stables. From Ambleside take A593 Coniston Road half a mile to Clappergate, sharp left to Hawshead on B5286 for just over a mile then right turn ,signposted Tarn Hows (unclassified road) for 2 ish miles, past Drunken Duck Inn, Yewfield is on right side

07924
179199

Beechmount

Near Sawrey, Hawkshead
Ambleside, Cumbria LA22 0JZ
Tel: 015394 36356 Fax:

3 rooms, 2 en suite, £19.50 pp, £130 weekly rate. All rooms have individual heating controls, t/v, hairdryer, radio etc. Guest lounge with t/v, video, stereo, books, games, maps and organ. Charming spacious country house with relaxed   friendly atmosphere. Breakfast is vegetarian wholefood and hearty

enough to fuel the walkers. In Beatrix Potter country with walks to the lakes, tarns, streams and spectacular hills. Esthwaite water a few minutes stroll away. No evening meal at the moment, good selection of pubs and restaurants offering veggie and vegan food in easy reach. On the B5285, from the north via Ambleside, from the south via Newby Bridge or there is a car ferry across Windermere

Garden Room Cafe

Zeffirellis Complex, Compston Road
Ambleside. Cumbria LA22 9DP
Tel: 015394 31612 Fax:
Open everyday 10.00-17.30
Vegetarian café in lovely Lakeland, Homemade soups,pates £1.95-£3.25. Salads £1.95-£3.50, daily specials e.g. polenta with sun dried tomatoes, hot filled baguettes, chillie, jacket potatoes, quiches etc. Usual desserts and an abundance of homemade cakes, slices and buns. Licenced.

Zeffirellis

Compston Road. Ambleside
Cumbria LA22 9AN
Tel: 015394 33845 Fax: 015394 31771
Mon-Fri 18.00-21.45, Sat & Sun 12.00-14.00, 17.00-21.45.
Italian vegetarian wholefood restaurant in complex with 2 screen cinema, shopping gallery and vegetarian café. Antipastas £1.95-£3.50 include soup, pate, roasted veggies, garlic mushrooms etc. Pizzas £4.95-£6.45. Mains £5.25-£6.50 such as ministra con fagiole, canneloni, chillie, pasta etc. plus daily specials. Desserts tiramasu, crème brulee, torte, frozen yog, and sorbet or fruit salad for vegans. House wine £7.95. Takeaway service for the pizzas.

Appleby in Westmoreland

The Friary

Battlebarrow, Appleby in Westmorland
Cumbria CA16 6XT
Tel: 017683 52702 Fax:
One twin and one double room, both en suite, £20 per person.
Spacious and comfortable accommodation is offered in grade
II listed Georgian Country home with self catering cottages sit-
uated in its own beech wood grounds, specialising in vegetari-
an cuisine. Vegetarian breakfast and they can make it vegan.
No other food provided.

Cockermouth

Quince and Medlar

13 Castlegate, Cockermouth
Cumbria CA13 9EU
Tel: 01900 823 579 Fax:
Tues-Sunday from 19.00 booking advisable
Twice winner of the Vegetarian Restaurant of the Year Award
and three times runner up. Situated in a listed Georgian building with a wood panelled candlelit dining room. Starters £2.95
for the soup to £3.65 for a salad of avocado & roasted beetroot. Main courses £7.95 include carrot & pea roulade, lentil &
apricot strudel, solyanka, terrine etc. Puddings £3.85 such as
chocolate orange pie, iced benedictine souffle, rhubarb ice
cream. Coffee with homemade choccies £1.25. Well worth
treating yourself.

Coniston

Beech Tree Guest House

Yewdale Road, Coniston
Cumbria LA21 8DX
Tel: 015394 41717 Fax:
3 double £18-£20, 2 en suite £24, 1 twin £19, 1 en suite £23, 1
family £50
This former Vicarage dating from the 18th century is set in its
own grounds and standing at the foot of the Old Man of
Coniston offers exclusively vegetarian cuisine. Tea/coffee in

rooms, TV lounge. No evening meal, but there's a large selection of places for veggie food in lovely Lakeland.
Directions: on Ambleside to Coniston Road 100 yards from the village centre.

Grange over Sands

Fernhill Vegetarian Country House

Fernhill, Witherslack
Grange over Sands, Cumbria LA11 6RX
Tel: 015395 52237 Fax: 015395 52237
FERNHILLV@AOL.com
1 single £22-24, 1 double en suite £44-48, 1 double with own bathroom £48-52.

Both doubles can be used as family rooms. All 3 rooms have wonderful views over the Winster valley. Evening meal from £7 for a seasonal meal eaten "en famile" or 4 course gourmet meal £18, vegans catered for, using local organic wholefood, home made preserves, packed lunches available. 5% discount for Veg & Vegan Society members. Leave M6 at junction 36, take A590 towards Windermere.

[handwritten: 015395 52367 Mike + Denise Key Moss B+B]

Grasmere

Eller Close

Eller Close House, Grasmere
Cumbria LA22 9RW
Tel: 015394 35786 Fax:
Self catering cottages.
Set in delightful secluded gardens just a few minutes walk from Grasmere village.

LEETWOOD
MONEY ADVICE CONSULTANTS
GROWING MONEY FOR GOOD

Ethical Investment Guide 1997/8

How do you know if your pension or investments are being managed effectively, and how do you compare the performance and ethical standing of the thousands of funds on offer?

Our unbiased guide to ethical investment funds is the only guide to give regularly updated performance figures and an ethical critique of all of the ethical funds. Furthermore, we can obtain discounts on the normal charges, so that it can be cheaper to go through us than to go direct to the company concerned. We also have a network of associates throughout the country who can advise you on a personal basis.

For more information and a free copy of the guide (not to be used in conjunction with other financial consultants) please return the coupon or contact :

Fleetwood M.A.C., **FREEPOST** NT2982, Garnett Bridge, Kendal LA8 9BR.
E-mail: john@fleetwood-mac.ymn.co.uk

24 HOUR FREEPHONE 0800 018 3041.

Associates in: Scotland. Yorkshire. Cumbria. Northern Ireland. Wales. West Midlands. East Midlands. Oxon. London. South West. South East. Sussex

Yes, please contact me. I am interested in:

☐ **Investment** ☐ **Pensions** ☐ **Life assurance** ☐ **Managed stockbroking** ☐ **Other** (please specify)

Amount available for investment: £ ....L.S./P.M.

Title: Mr/Mrs/Ms/Miss   Name: ....

Forename: ....

Tel. No. .... (Day) .... (Evening)

Address: ....

....

A member of DBS Financial Management PLC which
is regulated by the Personal Investment Authority

DBS

Dove Cottage Tea Rooms Restaurant

Town End, Grasmere
Cumbria LA22 9SH
Tel: 015394 35268 Fax: 015394 35268
Open every day 10.00-17.00, Fri & Sat 18.30-21.00
Vegetarian tea room in exquisite Grasmere, also restaurant
Friday and Saturday off season and most evenings during
summer, reservations recommended. Daytime soups from
£2.20, salads from £3.25. Pie, pasta and hot dish of day
£4.45-£5.50, rools, pate etc. Also gingerbread (local delicacy)
with hot toffee sauce £2.45. Scones of course, various cakes,
slices and shortbread. Evening menu 5 entrees £2.25-£3.95, 5
mains £7.50-£7.95 only 1 vegan. Home-made desserts £3.20
& house wine £8.

Lancrigg Vegetarian Country House Hotel & Restaurant

Easedale, Grasmere
Cumbria LA22 9QN
Tel: 015394 35317 Fax: 015394 35058
2 single £45-£70, 11 double & 2 twin £45-£90, 1 family all en-suite. All year.
Price includes 4 course dinner and breakfast. Non residents can also dine in, though booking essential, £20 with vegan option, 18.30-20.00. Historic farmhouse with "lakeland poets" connection, set in 30 acres of peaceful wooded gardens over-looking the valley of Easedale, Many rooms have special fea-tures such as four poster beds and whirlpool baths. All rooms have tv, tea/coffee and breakfast served in room if feeling indolent after last night's dinner. Also special rates for 3 night programmes. Half a mile from beautiful Grasmere, take junc-tion 36 from M6, A591 to Grasmere then turn left at village centre on the Easedale Road, half mile to Lancrigg.

The Rowan Tree

Church Bridge, Grasmere
Cumbria LA22 9SN
Tel: 01539 435 528 Fax:
Open: Spring-Autumn every day 10-17.00, 18-21.00.
Vegetarian café. Also open Fri-Sun day and evening in Winter till Xmas; then Jan-Feb just weekends daytime.

Hawkshead

A Room With a View

1st Floor, Laburnam House
The Square, Hawkshead
Cumbria LA22 0NZ
Tel: 015394 36 751 Fax:
Open everyday in summer, weekends in winter. 18.00-21.00
Vegetarian restaurant overlooking the pictuesque square in Hawkshead village. Menu changes fortnightly, starters £2.95-

£3.95 melon & orange salsa, mascarpone parfait etc. Mains £6.75-£7.50 hazelnut roast, leek & wensleydale roulade, terrine, all with salad bowl. Normally at least 1 vegan option and willing to adapt where possible. House wine £8.50.

Kendal

Fox Hall Vegan B&B & Self Catering

Sedgwick, Kendal, Cumbria LA8 0JP
Tel: 015395 61241 Fax: 015395 61241
1twin and 1double £17.50 per person.
Children under 5yrs free; 5-16 £10
Exclusively vegan catering and a warm and friendly atmosphere are offered in this converted 17th century barn. Dinner £10, packed lunches available. Also self-catering cottage which sleeps 4, £150-£260, with 2 bedrooms, kitchen, lounge and even own garage. Good local walks.
Directions: M6 junction 36, A590 for Barrow, at roundabout with A591 & A590 take last exit to Sedgwick, then 1 mile under canal bridge and it`s 1st house on left.

Lakeland Natural Vegetarian Guesthouse

Low Slack, Queens Road
Kendal, Cumbria LA9 4PH
Tel: 01539 733011 Fax: 01539 733011
Vegetarian guest house. 1 single £26-36, 3 double & 2 twin £26, all en suite, also 2 family rooms at £72. All rooms have TV, tea/coffee and also breakfast served in rooms if you're feeling indolent. Evening meal £12.50 with vegan option. A few minutes walk to centre of Kendal, a thriving market town.
Directions: enter Kendal from north on A5284, Queens Road is first right turn, house is at highest point on Queens Road.

Waterside Wholefoods

Kent View, Off Lowther Street
Waterside Kendal
Cumbria LA9 4PH
Tel: 01539 729 743 Fax: 01539 733 011
Mon-Thu 9.00-16.00, Fri 9.00-21.00, Sat 9.00-16.00 (Sun
10.00-16.00 summer only)
Vegetarian café and wholefood shop, also do outside catering.
Entrees £1.90-£2.65 normally 3 with at least one vegan, vari-
ous salads 90p a portion or £3.35 as course. Mains £2.05-£4
from choice of 3 casseroles, pies, bobbotie, roulade etc.
Choice of desserts and house wine £6.99.

Keswick

Eden Green

20 Blencathra St, Keswick, Cumbria CA12 4HP
Tel: 017687 72077
106143.1772@compuserve.com
1 single £17.50, 4 double £18-£23 3 en suite, 2 twin £18-£23,
1 family £23

Vegetarian, Victorian house close to town centre, most rooms
with mountain views, open all year. T/v, tea/coffee, hairdryer,
radio alarms in all rooms. Full English veggie breakfast, safe
cycle storage, children & dogs welcome. Also have themed
breaks, christmas & valentines special packages. Discounts for
Vegetarian & Vegan Society members.

The Lakeland Pedlar Wholefood Café
& Bicycle Centre.

Bell Close Car Park, Hendersons Yard
Keswick, Cumbria
Tel: 017687 74492 Fax: 017687 75202
Everyday 9.00-17.00, and till 20.00 during school hols.
Wholefood veggie restaurant popular with bikers, no, not the
big rough & hairy leather boys, the pedalists. Breakfast £1
muesli to £4.20 for fry up special. Starters £1.95-£3.25 soup,

hummous, nachos, boneshaker salad. Stuffed pittas, sandwiches & snacks during day. Mains £5-£6 chillie, burritos,
pasta, curry and a fun selction of pizzas. Desserts£2.55-£3.20
fruit salad, banoffi, cheesecake, sticky toffee etc. Fully
licenced.

Greenside

48 St John Street, Keswick-on-Derwentwater
Cumbria LA12 5AG
Tel: 017687 74491 Fax:
3 doubles all en suite £14-£17 all with self catering facilities.
Vegetarian Georgian house in the old part of Keswick with
views over the surrounding fells, 3 mins walk to town and 5
mins to shore of Derwentwater. Continental breakfast is
served at any time to suit, in your room which is also equipped
with full snack and packed lunch making facilities.Health food
shop and squillions of veggie restaurants, see other listings.

The Lakeland Pedlar

WHOLEFOOD CAFÉ-RESTAURANT

Keswick's only true vegetarian café-restaurant is an
ideal meeting place for a day out in the hills, a cycle
ride, shopping or simply a chat!

During the day our menu features a mouth watering
selection of home baked breads, cakes, pizzas, spicy
chillis and other sweet and savoury eats.

On selected evenings through out the year, we offer a
feast of imaginative vegetarian cuisine from around
the world - using nothing but the finest, freshest
ingredients...naturally.

With our relaxed non-smoking atmosphere, good music
fine views, tables outside, take-away service and OF
COURSE good food, we think you'll enjoy your visit.

THE LAKELAND PEDLAR WHOLEFOOD CAFÉ AND BICYCLE
CENTRE

Bell Close Car Park (just off the Market Square), Keswick.

Tel: 017687 - 74492

The Tea Rooms

39 Main Street, Kirkby Lonsdale
Cumbria LA6 2AH
Tel: 015242 72133 Fax:
Mon-Sat 9.00-17.00. Sun 10.00-17.00
Café and tea room offering some vegetarian selections. Offers 10% discount to Vegetarian and Vegan Society members and Viva! members.

Chestnut House

Crosby Garrett, Kirkby Stephen
Cumbria CA17 4PR
Tel: 017683 71230 Fax:
Omnivorous guest house. 1 double, 1 family £16.50 pp per night, open all year.
A relaxed and tranquil atmosphere is promised in this traditional cottage in a small quiet village off the beaten track in the secluded upper Eden Valley. Vegetarian or vegan evening meal £10, packed lunch £3-£3.75. No TV so peace and quiet main attraction, quiet lanes and footpaths for walkers. Near Settle to Carlisle railway, good base for exploring Swaledale, Wensleydale, Teesdale and Howgill Fells. Off A685.

Lupton Tower

Lupton, Nr Kirkby Lonsdale
Cumbria LA6 2PR
Tel: 01539 567400 Fax:
1 double £22, 4 double en suite £28-£35, 1 twin £28. Open all year.
Vegetarian country house hotel, tea/coffee, washbasin in rooms. Veg or vegan evening meal £19.50. On A65 2 miles from east from junction 36 of M6, 3 miles from Kirkby Lonsdale.

The Watermill Tearoom

Little Salkeld, Nr Penrith
Cumbria CA10 1NN
Tel: 01768 881523 Fax:
Mon-Tue & Thurs 10.00-17.00. March-Oct. Mill tours 11.00-
12.00, 14.30-15.30.

Tearoom overlooking Sunnygill Beck, next to organic watermill with shop selling flours and dried goods, as well as guided tours of the Mill. Also run breadmaking, jam-making, baking and veggie cooking courses. Soup, veggie tart, millers lunch (ploughman), for around £3. Puddings £2.25 and cakes, scones etc. with wide choice of teas. You`d need strong willpower to resist eating with the home baking smells wafting by.

Wigton

The Watermill Restaurant

Priests Mill, Caldbeck
Wigton, Cumbria CA7 8DR
Tel: 016974 78267 Fax:
Open everyday 10.00-17.00, Monday 11.00-16.00, closed
Mondays Oct-Jan

Vegetarian restaurant using freshly made local produce, light refreshments to full meals. Some tables overlook the river or you can sit outside on the grassy terrace overlooking the village cricket pitch. Situated in Priests Mill an 18th century stone building, which also houses a gift shop, a goldsmith and bric-a-brac shop.Secluded position almost hidden from road.

Vegetarian Guides make perfect prezzies.
Britain, France, Oz/NZ, World and more to come....
See the order form at the end of this book.

SCOTLAND

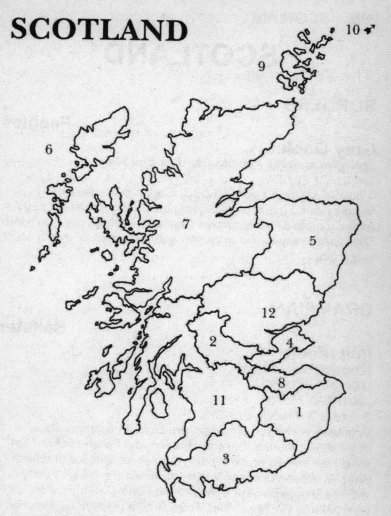

1. BORDERS
2. CENTRAL SCOTLAND
3. DUMFRIES & GALLOWAY
4. FIFE
5. GRAMPIAN
6. HEBRIDES
7. HIGHLANDS
8. LOTHIAN
9. ORKNEY
10. SHETLAND
11. STRATHCLYDE
12. TAYSIDE

SCOTLAND

BORDERS

Peebles

Grey Gables
Springwood Road, Peebles, Borders EH45 9HB
Tel: 01721 721252
1 double & 1 twin from £16 B&B, Easter to September
Veggie owned guest house, going totally vegetarian for 1999.
Evening meal £7.50 is always vegetarian, bring your own wine.
Directions: easy to find once you get to Peebles or they'll send
you a map.

GRAMPIAN

Ballater

Inverdeen
Bridge Square, Ballater
Grampian AB3 5QJ
Tel: 01339 755759
2 double & 1 family £18-£30
Vegetarian or vegan breakfast available. In cosmopolitan
antique filled house, German, French and Polish spoken. Set
amid pine forests and mountains, great for outdoor pursuits.
From Aberdeen direction when you reach the bridge junction
with the village on your right and the River Dee bridge on left,
Inverdeen is straight ahead. From Braemar/Balmoral direction
go through village past the Kirk (church) Green, when road
takes hard left for Aberdeen or straight on for bridge Inverdeen
is on right. Also 2 mins from bus station.

Castle Of Park

Cornhill, Banffshire AB4 2AX
Tel: 01466 751667
4 private suites £28-£35 some with 4 poster beds.
Veggie friendly 16th century castle. Private suites or they do house parties if you are taking a big group, tel for details. Near coast. Veg breakfast options, and restaurant, open to non residents, with 3 course dinner about £12 from veg menu.

Gordon Arms Hotel

Kincardine O`Neil, Royal Deeside
Grampian AB52 6QT
Tel: 01467 620981
5 double & 2 family rooms £22.50-£55
Veggie friendly hotel and bar, formerly coaching inn. Bar snacks and vegetarian options on lunch & dinner menus, hot food from 11.30-14.30 & 17.00-21.00.

Quince Cottage

72 Findhorn, Forres
Grampian IV36 0YF
Tel: 01309-690495
Omnivorous bed and breakfast in a traditional stone-built old cottage by the sea, with lots of pine inside and a wood burning stove. 1 double £30, 1 twin en suite £36 per person, can be let as singles £17-50 and £20. Veggie and vegan breakfasts available using the finest ingredients from the local Findhorn wholefood shop such as organic bread, veggie sausages, organic baked beans.

Helios Café

Findhorn Foundation, The Park, Findhorn
Forres, Grampian IV30 0TZ
Tel: 01309 091301
Mon-Sat 10.00-17.00, Sun 11.00-17.00

Vegetarian café serving organic wholefood at the famous
Findhorn. Big selection of tea, coffee, juices and non-caffeines
from 50p. Scones, fruit bread, croissant, flapjacks, pastries
60p-£1.25. Toasted sandwiches, baked potatoes, baguettes,
pie, pizza, pasties etc. £1.95-£2.50. There's also a wholefood
shop nearby and bookshop selling the kind of books you'd
hope to find in Findhorn plus tapes, crafts, and an apothecary
in the store......

Minton House

Findhorn, Forres, Moray
Grampian IV36 0YY
Tel: 01309 690819 Fax: 01309 691583
1 single, 7 double £17-£32

Vegetarian Hotel next to Findhorn. Big pink mansion on the
bay shore set in 6 acres of grounds. Veggie breakfast and
evening meal £7. Run as a retreat centre with various workshops held in the ballroom, also offers hot tub & sauna at
week ends, massage, yoga etc. Area of outstanding beauty.
Via the A9 Edinburgh to Inverness then A96 Inverness to
Forres, then follow the signs to Findhorn. Also bus or rail services to Forres.

Neptune Guest House & Verdant Restaurant

22/24 Tolbooth Street, Forres
Morayshire IV36 0PH
Tel: 01309 674387 Fax: 01309 674387
2 single (1 en suite) £18.50-£20, 1 double, 1 twin & I family all
en suite £35,

Vegetarian with tea/coffee, t/v and breakfast in rooms. Full breakfast and evening meal £10 for three courses, also extensive snacks menu for when the nibblies strike. Excellent choice of beers, wines and spirits. Leave A96 Aberdeen-Inverness road at 1st roundabout for Forres, road leads to High St, turn into Tolbooth St and Neptune House is 200 yards on right.

HIGHLANDS & ISLANDS

Kingussie

Sonnhalde

East Terrace, Kingussie
Highlands PH21 1JS
Tel: 01540 661266 Fax: 01540 661266
7 double (4 en suite) £18-£21 Jan-October
Veggie friendly , victorian villa on a sunny bank (if you`re lucky) just above the High St. with a splendid view across the Spey valley overlooked by the Cairngorn mountains. Hill walking, skiing, the Highland Folk Museum, the Whiskey Trail etc. Evening meal £9.

Newtonmore

Craigellachie House

Main St, Newtonmore
Highlands PH20 1DA
Tel: 01540 673360
2 family rooms from £16 pp
Veggie friendly.

UNIQUE HIGHLANDS B&B

Stay on a first class train
beside ScotRail station on Inverness-Wick line

Rogart Station
Sutherland Scotland

From £13 PER PERSON
10% Reduction for rail users and cyclists

Tel or fax Kate/Frank 01408 641343
e-mail rograil@globalnet.co.uk

Onich

Cuildraig House

Onich, Nr Fort William
Highlands PH3 6SD
Tel: 01855 821529
2 double , 1 family £15-£18 January-November.
Vegetarian, breakfast only in summer, dinner usually available
in winter for £10. Spectacular scenery with walking, climbing,
cycling and skiing in winter. Take A82 Glasgow road, about 8
miles south of Fort William.

Sutherland

Achins Coffee Shop

Inverkirkaig, Lochinver
Sutherland IV27 4LS
Tel: 01571 844 262 Fax: 01571 844 262
Everyday 10.00-17.00 from Easter -October.
Small vegetarian coffee shop with a limited menu. Soup £1.60,
baked potatoes & salad £3.75, toasted sandwiches, nut roast,
quiche etc. Breads and rolls all home baked.

Rogart Railway Carriage Co

Station House, Rogart, Sutherland IV28 3XA
Tel: 01408 641343
All year in house or March-November in carriages.
It`s a train, with 8 doubles in the carriages £10.50-£15, 1 twin
en suite (in the house) £15-£17 and self contained hostel
£8.50. Also a 10% discount for rail users and cyclists.
Wonderful place for train lovers or a"brief encounter," sounds
like a fun idea. Local attractions are hill walking or cycling in
the lovely Scottish countryside, drinking pints of heavy.
Vegetarian 3 course dinner £8. Directions, get off the train at
Rogart or A9 north from Inverness then A839 towards Lairg
and Rogart.

More **MEMBERS** Means
More **CAMPAIGNING** Means
More **SUCCESS**

Thanks to membership contributions we are able to campaign strongly for a more compassionate, environmentally–conscious and healthier world.

Our recent successes include:

- Highlighting the link between red meat consumption and increased incidence of cancer
- The banning of 'exotic' meats such as kangaroo and ostrich from supermarket shelves
- Raising awareness of environmental destruction caused by meat and fish production

We are also able to keep vegetarian issues in the headlines, increase the amount of choice available and provide information to help five thousand other people a week in the UK go veggie.

Just imagine what we could achieve with your support?

Join The Vegetarian Society today and you could also enjoy discounts in thousands of shops, health food stores, restaurants and holiday destinations. Our members hotline and fact–packed magazine — 'The Vegetarian' —means whatever you want to know, we'll provide the answers. We'll also give you enough recipe ideas to keep your taste buds tingling!

For vegetarians everywhere, membership of the Society is essential. Call us on **0161 928 0793** for a free starter pack.

Vegetarian
SOCIETY

Registered Charity No. 259358

The Ceilidh Place

14 West Argyle Street, Ullapool IV26 2TY
tel 01854612103 fax 01854612886

Hotel : Bookshop : Restaurant : Concerts

Coffee shop : Performance : Bar :

Exhibitions : Courses : Clubhouse

Open All Year

Ullapool

The Ceilidh Place

14 West Argyle Street, Ullapool
Wester Ross, Highlands IV26 2TY
Tel: 01854 612103 Fax: 01854 612886
In the hotel £50, bunk house £15
Veggie friendly hotel, restaurant, coffee shop and concert
venue in the West Highland village of Ullapool. Most rooms
have private facilities and all have telephones. Tea and coffee
making in the residents' lounge, which overlooks Loch Broom
and has superb views of the surrounding mountains. There is
also a courtesy bar from which you can help yourself to a
reviving drink after a day out walking, climbing or just enjoying
the West Highland scenery. They have a bookshop and art
exhibitions regularly, plus summer programme of entertainments ranging from traditional Scottish to jazz to classical.

Glem Frulart

3 Castle Terrace, Ullapool
Wester Ross, Highlands IV26 2XD
Tel: 01854 612409
April-October 1 single, I twin & 1 double en suite £13-£18.
Vegetarian b and b. in bungalow overlooking the sea. Local
attractions include Bird Island, hill walking, swimming pool etc.
From south arrive at pierhead in Ullapool, take right up hill 500
meters to T junction, take right over river then 4th house on
left.

Taigh Na Mara Vegan Guest House

The Shore, Ardindrean, Lochbroom
Nr Ullapool, Highlands IV23 2SE
Tel: 01854-655282 Fax: 01854-655292
mara@lochness.co.uk
Open all year, booking essential
Britain's top vegan guest house with superb gourmet food, per-
fect for a peaceful getaway to recharge your batteries. One
twin , one double and one double en suite honeymoon bed-

room, £35-40 per person including dinner. Full Scottish vegan breakfast. Evening meal £15 available to non-residents featuring top class vegan cuisine with a Scottish flavour. Check out the luxury vegan cookbook Rainbows and Wellies by the Taigh Na Mara chef to see just what delights await you. You can bring your own booze. 5% discount for VSUK, Vegan Soc, Viva!, PETA, Animal Aid. High chairs.

Islay

Ceol-na-mara

Bruichladdich, Islay PA49 7UN
Tel: 01496 850371
2 doubles and 1 twin from £17.
Vegetarian b&b though evening meal can be arranged for £10. Guest lounge with t/v available all day. 10 metres from the Loch shore on the charming Islay, the most southerly of the Hebridean islands. A soft climate due to the Gulf Stream, even in winter. Miles of dunes, sandy beaches and cliffs, you`re likely to see seals, otters, deer, golden eagles and hen harriers. Walking, trekking, surfing diving and a heated swimming pool on the island, and the famous single malts from the distilleries, though beware a "wee dram" seems to mean about a half pint of whiskey! There are two flights a day from Glasgow or buses from Buchanan St bus station (in Glasgow) which connect with the mid-day & evening ferry, takes three and a half hours. By car M8 then A83 (Campbeltown) to Tarbert then A83 passing Loch Fyne. 5 miles south of Tarbert is Caledonian Mac Braynes Ferries terminal of Kennacraig, crossing 2 hours.

Isle of Skye

Glamaig View B&B

5 Bosville Terrace, Portree
Isle of Skye IV51 9DG
Tel: 01478 612 152
1 double en suite £16-£21, 1 family en suite £15-£18 both with views.
Vegetarian b&b with restaurant (see Ben Tianavaig), t/v and tea/coffee in rooms. On the wonderful Isle of Skye with all it`s

scenic delights. Out of village towards Staffin overlooking Portree harbour.

Ben Tianavaig Vegetarian Bistro

5 Bosville Terrace, Portree
Isle of Skye IV51 9DG
Tel: 01478-612 152
Open: Tue-Sun 18.00-21.30, closed Mon.
Open in season only.

Vegetarian restaurant (also b&b at same address) with a mixture of cuisines which are mainly vegan. 3 vegan and 2 veggie entrées £4.50 such as stuffed aubergine or falafel. Side salads and 7 mains at £7.95 cashew nut roast, kebabs, pasta etc. Puddings vary depending on cooks mood, invariably a good mood you`ll be glad to hear. Litre of wine £8.50.

Donmar

43 Bernisdale, Isle of Skye
Isle of Skye IV51 9NS
Tel: 01470 532204
2 family rooms £17 per adult.
Vegetarian, near Portree. 10% VSUK and Vegan Society members.

Kensalroag House

Dunvegan, Isle of Skye IV55 8GZ
Tel: 01470 521306
1 single, 1 twin, 1 double from £15. April-November.
Vegetarian/vegan. 2 mins from sea. Dinner £12.

Quiraing Lodge

Staffin, Isle of Skye IV51 9JS
Tel: 01470 562330
1 double & 6 twin (2 family) £17
Vegetarian family home, caters for all diets. Sitting room, library, sanctuary, most with stoves or open fires. Overlooking spectacular Skye shoreline. Packed lunches, dinner for just £8.50 Also bike hire available.

LOTHIAN

Edinburgh

No. 1

1 Gayfield Place
Edinburgh EH7 4AB
Tel: 0131 557 4752
1 single, 1 twin, 2 double £20-£25
Vegan & vegetarian, 10 minutes from Princes St. train and bus stations.

Six Mary's Place

Edinburgh's Superior Guest House

Beautifully restored Georgian townhouse in the heart of the city
offering vegetarian and vegan cuisine in a smoke free environment.
Delightful dining conservatory and gardens. Only five minutes
walk from the celebrated Royal Botanic Gardens and ideally
situated for everything Edinburgh has to offer.

Scottish Tourist Board Two Crown Commended status.

Contact: Elaine Gale, Six Mary's Place, Raeburn Place,
Stockbridge, Edinburgh EH4 1JH
Tel: 0131 332 8965, Fax: 0131 624 7060

Email: 100771.3705@compuserve.com
http://ourworld.compuserve.com/homepages/ECT_Social_Firms/smp1.htm

Six Marys Place

6 Marys Place, Raeburn Place
Stockbridge, Edinburgh EH4 1JH
Tel: 0131 332 8965
3 single & 3 double £28-£30, 2 twin en suite £32-£35
Vegetarian. With tea/coffee and t/v in room if requested, also t/v lounge. Usual veggie breakfasts and 3 course dinner for £9 which can be veganized. Just a few minutes from Princes St. Also 5% discount for VSUK members.

Bann's Vegetarian Cafe

5 Hunter Square, Edinburgh EH1 1QW
Tel: 0131 226 1112 Fax: 0131-226 1112
All 7 days 10.00-23.00
At least half menu is vegan. Veggie breakfast £5, starters from £1.75 include bruschetta, pates, hummous, bhajis, etc up to £5 for a tostada (tortillas with salsa, re-fried beans, tomato & mozzarella). Baked potatoes, and various croissant. Mains £5-£7.50 chilli, curry, veggie haggis, burgers, enchilladas, nut parcels etc. Selection of saladsas mains or sides. Selection of enticing desserts from £2.20 and house wine £7.40.

Black Bo's

57-61 Blackfriars Street, Edinburgh EH1 1NB
Tel: 0131 557 6136
Mon-Sat lunch & 18.00 21.30
Adventurous vegetarian food.

Helios Fountain

7 Grassmarket, Edinburgh EH1 2HY
Tel: 0131-229 7884 Fax: 0131-622 7173
Wholefood vegetarian café.

Henderson's Salad Table

94 Hanover Street, Edinburgh EH2 1DR
Tel: 0131 225 2131
Mon-Sat 8.00-late, Sun 10.00-22.00.
Vegetarian. Porridge, muesli, croissant, toast etc. 95p-£1.95 for breakfast. All day menu includes soup, burgers, patties, pasties, quiches, pizza £1.20-£2.20. Selection of 16 salads. Typical mains are nut loaf, risotto, souffle, stuffed aubergine, lentil lasagne etc. £3.50. Various desserts from £1.70. Local real ales, wines etc. Live music ranging from Jazz to Scottish Folk every evening from 19.30.

Isabel's Café

Underneath Nature's Gate
83 Clerk Street, Edinburgh EH8 9JG
Tel: 0131 662 4014
Mon-Sat 11.30-18.30 closed Sunday.
Wholefood vegan and vegetarian café. Starters £1.50-£2.25 soup, burger, hummous etc. 3 salads, Mains £3.50 kebabs, pasta, stuffed marrow, crumble, haggis with neeps & tatties, baked potatoes etc. Desserts £1.45-£1.75 plum crumble, apple pie, baked bananas, chocolate cake.

The Engine Shed Cafe

19 St Leonards Lane, Edinburgh EH8 9SD
Tel: 0131 662 0040
Open Mon-Thur 10.30-15.30;Fri 10.30-14.30; Sat10.30-16.00; Sun11.00-16.00.
Vegetarian café run by charitable organization. Soup 85p, salads 65p a selection. Mains such as roast veg & cous cous, lasagne, baked spuds £1.95. Vegan desserts like apple crumble or friut salad £1-£1.25. Tea 60p and coffee 65p. Remarkable value.

Cornerstone Cafe
St John's Church, Off Princes Street
Lothian Road, Edinburgh EH2 4BJ
Tel: 0131 229 0212
Mon-Sat 9.30-16.00 closed Sunday.
Veggie café, offering soups, 10 salads. Mains from leek pie, lasagne, pasta, cassoulet, crepes, hot pot, Thai rice dish etc. Home made cakes, tarts and pastries.
Prices not known.

The Baked Potato Shop
56 Cockburn Street, Edinburgh EH1 1PB
Tel: 0131 225 7572
Mon-Sun 9.00-21.00
Vegetarian and vegan tattie shop with loads of fillings from £2.30. Veg kebabs £1.60. Salads, soups and desserts as well.

Kalpna
2-3 St Patrick Square, Edinburgh EH8 9EZ
Tel: 0131 667 9890
Mon-Fri 11-14.00 & 17.30-23.00, Sat 17.30-23.00 closed Sun
Indian vegetarian . Starters £2-£3.50 pakoras, dosa masala, utapa etc. Mains £3.95-£7.50 from a more unusal menu include dam aloo Kashmire and those wonderful thalis, do try aloo bangara which has a very lively Rajastani sauce, only for the brave. Kulfis, gulab jaman, gajar halwa (carrot based with almonds and cardomans), sorbets etc. all at £2. Wine from £7.95. Also 5% discount for VSUK and Vegan Society members.

Susie`s Wholefood Diner
51/53 West Nicholson Street, Edinburgh E8 9DB
Tel: 0131 667 9729 Fax:
Mon-Sat 9.00-21.00, Sunday 13.00-20.00 in season.
Vegetarian with big vegan choice. With a counter service sys-

tem you can make combinations from the hot and cold coun-
ters as well as the made to order dishes. 2 soups at £1.70. For
mains a medium dish is £3.30-£3.65, large £4.30-£4.50 typical
dishes are cashew flan, stir fry, bean stew, lasagne, butterbean
croquettes, pizza, quiches etc. 6 salads and big selection of
desserts. House wine £5.

STRATHCLYDE

Ayrshire

The Old Sawmill Cottage

Kilkerran Estate, Crosshill
Maybole, Ayrshire KA19 7PZ
Tel: 01655 740451 Fax:
1 double en suite £15
Veg and vegan. In the midst of Rabbie Burns country, lots of
good walking nearby.

Glasgow

The 13th Note Cafe/Bar

50-60 King Street, Glasgow G1
Tel: 0141 553 1638 Fax: 0141 552 5797
Open Mon-Sat 08.00-23.45, Sun 12.30-23.45
Superb vegan café, restaurant and bar with take-away. Mixture
of European (slight Greek emphasis) and Asian foods.
Staggeringly extensive menu with 10 entrées £1.50-3.00 e.g.
dolmades (stuffed vine leaves); aubergine dip+pittta. 7 salads
£1.50-2.00 e.g. Greek or 'low fat'. 25 (yep, twenty-five) main
courses £3.50-6.00 such as Cashew Korma and poppadums;
Mezethes (assorted Greek starters); spinach + 'cream cheese'
dumplings; Veggie Loaf (recommended!); Stuffed peppers. At
least 5 desserts £2-3 include various ice creams, cheesecake
with amazing topppings, banoffi pie. House wine starts at
£7.50, glass £1.50. Teas 60p, Coffee 80p. 10% discount for
Vegan Society members. Non-smoking area. 80 seats.
Wheelchair access. Highchairs for children. If you're a
veg(etari)an then this place is the business.

Asha Vegetarian Restaurant
141 Elderslie Street
Glasgow G3 6JA
Tel: 0141 221 7144 Fax:
Mon-Sat 12.00-14.30 & 17.30-23.30, Sun 17.00-23.30.
Indian vegetarian and wholemeal restaurant. Patra, samosa, bhajis, pakora, kachori etc. £1.50-£2.25. Curry variations £3.50-£4.95, set meal options.

The Bay Tree
403 Great Western Road, Kelvinbridge
Glasgow G4 9HY
Tel: 0141 334 5898 Fax:
Everyday 8.00-21.00
Middle Eastern vegetarian cuisine.

Cafe Alba
Otago Street, Off Great Western Road
Kelvinbridge, Glasgow
Tel: 0141 337 2282 Fax:
Mon-Sat 10.00-17.00 closed Sunday.
Mainly vegetarian café with big cakes selection. Also soup, veggie burgers, quiche, lasagne, etc.

Vegville
St Georges Road, Charing Cross
Glasgow G3 6JA
Tel: 0141 333 1771 Fax: 0141 333 1648
Mon 11.30-18.30, Tue & Wed 11.30-21.00, Thu-Sat 11.30-23.00 closed Sunday
Vegetarian daytime fun & funky menu includes soup, burgers £1.35, jalapeno sausage in a hoagie £1.35, toasted soul food sandwiches, super sub, Elvis BLT, potato & leek bake, lasagne, tacos, tofu with noodles, tortillas, etc £2.95-£3.35.

Evening menu has choice of 6 starters £1.95-£3.45. Mains include tortillas, Shanghai stir fry, tagliatelli or gnocchi, tortellini, haggis with whiskey galore, pistachio & spinach etc. £5.25-£6.95.

Renfrewshire

East Lochhead

East Lochhead, Largs Road
Lochwinnoch, Renfrewshire PA12 4DX
Tel: 01505-842610 Fax: 01505-842610
Winnoch@aol.com
East Lochhead is a large Scottish farmhouse commanding beautiful views to the south east over the Barr Loch and Renfewshire hills, with 2 acres of gardens which guests are welcome to wander and enjoy, set within 25 acres of farmland. Situated one mile west of Lochwinnoch on the road to Largs it is close to Glasgow Airport and an ideal base for visiting Glasgow and touring Ayrshire, the Clyde coast, the Trossachs (Rob Roy country) and Loch Lomond. Omnivorous guesthouse with 1 twin with private bath & 1 family en suite £30 bed and veggie breakfast. Proprietor Janet Anderson is an enthusiastic (omnivorous) cook and a 3 course vegetarian dinner may be ordered by giving prior notice for around £18.
Also 3 cottages converted from barns, sleeping 2, 3-5 or 4-6 from £150-£480 per week depending on season.

TAYSIDE

Kinloch Rannoch

Glenrannoch

Kinloch Rannoch, Tayside PH16 5QA
Tel: 01882 632307 Fax:
1 twin & 2 double £18.50 or £32 with dinner.
Vegetarian and organic where possible. Situated at the eastern end of Loch Rannoch, the view is dominated by Schiehallion (the Fairy Mountain). Books and games in the lounge for cosy evenings or wet afternoons. Big range of wildlife in the unspoilt glen, red deer, red squirrels, pine martin,

wildcats, ospreys and eagles. Also evening meal available. Also near to West Highland Line, Blair Castle and Pitlochry Festival Theatre. Approx. 2 hours from Edinburgh and Glasgow, take A9 Perth to Inverness Road, then B8019 1 mile north of Pitlochry then follow signs for Kinloch Rannoch. In the village turn left opposite Dunalastair Hotel, cross narrow bridge over River Tummel. Next right signposted South Loch Road and Rannoch School wiill take you to Glenrannoch about 400 metres.

WESTERN ISLES (HEBRIDES)

Iona

Argyll Hotel

Isle of Iona, Western Isles PA76 6SJ
Tel: 01681 700334 Fax: 01681 700510
8 single, 9 twins & doubles most en suite £56-£60 includes dinner.
Seashore hotel with veggie friendly menu, price includes 3 course dinner with coffee etc.

Lewis

The Willows Vegetarian Guest House

19 Tolsta Chaolais
Isle of Lewis
Western Isles HS2 9DW
Tel: 01851 621321 Fax:
1 twin with own bathroom & lounge £18-£20
Full breakfast and evening meal for £12. On the Lochside with the beach, walking, climbing, Callanish Stones and all the space, peace and quiet you could want. On the west coast, telephone for directions when you book.

Mull

Bruach Mhor

Fionnphort, Isle of Mull
Western Isles PA66 6BL
Tel: 01681 700276 Fax:
1 single, 1 twin, 2 double £15 all with tea/coffee.
Vegetarian though if you have a confirmed carnivore with you
they will oblige them. Crofthouse on slopes of Tor Mor 5 mins
from the Iona ferry terminal, worth a visit to the famous Abbey.
Packed lunches £3 and dinner for £9 using home grown organic produce. Local boats do trips to Staffa to see the basalt
columns rising from the sea and to Lunga with its colonies of
guillemots, razorbills and those cute little puffins Ferry from
Oban to Craignure (about 45 mins), from Craignure take A849
along the Ross of Mull passing through Glen More to
Fionnphort, also buses meet some of the ferries. Via Fort
William or Glencoe A82 to the Corran-Ardgour ferry (5 min
crossing, no booking necessary) then A849.

Kyle of Lochalsh

Culag

Carr Brae, Dornie, Kyle of Lochalsh
Western Isles IV40 8HA
Tel: 01599 555341 Fax:
1 twin & 1 double en suite £16-£17.50
Vegan but will provide cow`s milk if requested. In an area of
outstanding beauty with mountains and a gorgeous coastline.
Big hearty vegan breakfast and 3 course dinner for £9.50.

Seagreen Restaurant and Bookshop

Plockton Road, Kyle of Lochalsh
Western Isles IV40 8DA
Tel: 01599 534 388 Fax:
Mon-Sun 10.00-17.00 Winter, till 21.00 in Summer.
Upmarket seafood restaurant with reasonable veggie selection.
2 entrees £1.70-£2.65. 3 mains strudel, bean burger, lasagne,
veg pie £4.25-£5.50. Desserts £3.95.

WALES

1. CLWYD
2. DYFED
3. MID GLAMORGAN
4. SOUTH GLAMORGAN
5. WEST GLAMORGAN
6. GWENT
7. GWYNEDD & ANGLESEY
8. POWYS

Due to the confusion created by the renaming of counties in Wales, we have used both the original name and the new name, which is usually the previous original name. Confused? Us too, and young Alex even went to a Welsh speaking school in Barry.

1. Clwyd is now Denbighshire
2. Dyfed is now Pembrokeshire
6. Gwent is now Monmouthshire
8. Powys is now Montgomery

Gwynedd and the Glamorgans stay the same - for the present.

WALES

DYFED (PEMBROKESHIRE)

Carmarthen

Waverley Vegetarian Restaurant

23 Lammas Street
Carmarthan, Dyfed SA31 3AL
Tel: 01267 236 521 Fax:
Open: Mon-Sat 9-17.00
Vegetarian and vegan café where you can eat for £3 and up.
Teas from 50p.

Fishguard

Coach House Cottage

Glendower Square, Goodwick
Fishguard, Dyfed SA64 0DH
Tel: 01348 873660 Fax:
Omnivorous guest house. Traditional Pembrokeshire cottage
offering vegetarian fare, set in a secluded location 5 minutes
walk from Fishguard Harbour and the seafront. 1 twin room,
£13.50 per person per night. No evening meal, but there are
plenty of places nearby with veggie food. Cooked breakfast
and they always have soya milk available.

Gwaun Valley

Tregynon Country Farmhouse Hotel

Gwaun Valley, near Fishguard
Pembrokeshire SA65 9TU
Tel: 01239 820531 Fax: 01239 820808
Tregynon@compuserve.com
Restaurant open every night 19.30-20.30. Hotel closed 2
weeks in winter.
Award winning omnivorous 16th century hotel set in the foot

hills of the Preseli mountains and surrounded by unspoilt countryside with an abundance of wildlife. 2 doubles £30-32, 2 family £34, 2 four poster £36, all prices per person. Children sharing with two adults 8-10 years £17, 11-13 £20. Rooms in main farmhouse or cottage, all en suite. Includes full English vegetarian or vegan breakfast. TV and tea/coffee making in rooms. Bar. Packed lunches £6.50. Weekly £320-360 per person. Xmas to Boxing Day (3 nights minimum over Christmas) £63-39 per person, 27-30 Dec normal prices, New Year's eve add £10 to Xmas price. Great little breaks 1st Nov 98-31 Mar 99 including evening dinner two days £90-102pp, three days £132-150pp.

Omnivorous gourmet restaurant which has catered for vegetarians for 17 years. If you stay for two weeks you'll discover that they do not repeat a vegetable cooked in the same way (including potatoes) for 15 days! Prior booking is essential and to discuss what is available that day. Set price policy £18.95 (£19.45 for non-residents) for full meal including coffee. 3 or 4 vegetarian (but not vegan) entrées and 1 main such as tomato roulade. All desserts are veggie. There's almost nothing vegan, but dishes are available by prior arrangement. An alternative vegetarian main course is offered daily for £3 supplement, such as brazil nut and craberries wrapped in puff pasty with cranberry and Madeira sauce; or stuffed pancake with tomato and Moscatel sauce. House wine £10.50, glass £1.95. Tea £1.25, coffee £1.30, soya milk. If you bring your own wine there is a corkage charge £5.

Directions: at crossroads with B4329, take B4313 towards Fishguard. First right and first right again then 1.5 mils on left. OS map 145, ref 054345.

Haverfordwest

Hilton Mill
Roch, Haverfordwest
Pembrokeshire SA62 6AE
Tel: 01437 710744 Fax:

Mallards is a totally self-contained luxury aparment, vegetarian owned, on the ground floor of a converted three-storey stone watermill built in 1851. Bookings Sat-Sat £110-245 per week. Set in 6 acres of partially wooded grounds kept as a nature reserve. The flat comprises sitting/dining room, superb kitchen, shower room with washbasin and toilet, and lobby. Microwave, electric cooker, fridge, washing machine, colour TV, electric heating. Use of tumble dryer in stable. £1 electric slot meter. Bed linen provided (duvet), bring your own towels and tea towels. No children under 10. As the apartment only sleeps two (double bed) it is really only suitable for a couple or single person. Regret no pets due to resident animals and ducks. No smoking.

The millpond nearby attracts much wildlife including heron, kingfisher, moorhens and mallard ducks. There is a small enclosed coutyard with garden furniture and an area by the old waterwheel which is a pleasant suntrap. Badges, foxes, squir-rels, rabbits and very many species of birds are the neigh-bours in this peaceful, unspoilt paradise. 3 miles from Newgale beach in St Brides Bay, a region of spectacular coastal scenery with many rocky inlets, quiet coves and beach-es, dotted with small islands which teem with colonies of seabirds. Close to the Preseli mountains, watersports and coastal path walking.

Directions: A487 through Simpson Cross village until last prop-erty on left, which is a small lodge adjacent to the end 40mph signs. Turn left here, between stone pillars, down country lane, through woods. Hilton Mill is on the left when lane levels out after 2/3 mile.

The Old Court House

Trefin, Nr St Davids, Haverfordwest
Pembrokeshire SA62 5AX
Tel: 01348 837095 Fax:
Open all year

Vegetarian guest house and restaurant that caters well for vegans in a 200 year old cosy cottage, tastefully decorated with open fires. 1 family en suite, 1 double en suite, 1 single/bunk, £18.50-19.50. Under 5 free, 5-11 £% B&B, 11-15 half price if sharing, children's meals negotiable. Tea/coffee making and TV. Range of hearty full English veggie or vegan breakfasts with lashings of wholemeal toast. Sitting room with open fire, books and CDs. Central heating. South facing garden with children's play area. Evening meal £12.50 in their restaurant open to non-residents. 5% discount for VSUK and Vegan Society. No smoking in the cottage. Well behaved child-friendly dogs are welcome by arrangement. Packed lunches made freshly to order £3.50.

Three course evening meals are prepared by Lynne, a Cordon Vert chef, using local produce served in their beautiful dining room. Sample menu is garlic mushrooms in filo parcels, then spinach and lentil roulade with spicy tomato sauce followed by apricot and almond upside down pudding with cashew custard, then tea or coffee. Bring your own wine if you wish.

7 nights dinner, B&B £197, or £247 with 5 days self-guided walking and packed lunched. 2-3 day short breaks £60-108. Off season discounts.

Situated halfway between St Davids and Fishguard in a small coastal village just off A487, on the main street opposite the old chapel. Or take the train to Haverfordwest or Fishguard where they'll meet you. 5 minutes walk from Pembrokeshire coast footpath, within a national park, close to the ferry to Ireland. OS grid ref 838325.

Rosebush

The Old Post Office

Rosebush, Pembrokeshire SA66 7QU
Tel: 01437 532205 Fax:
Restaurant open Mon-Fri 10-23.00, Sat 10-24.00,
Sun 10-17.00

Omnivorous hotel and restaurant open to non-residents, with masses for vegetarians, half of it vegan. Two doubles and one single, £17.95 per person per night. Tea/coffee making, wash-basins and TV in rooms. Cooked vegan or veggie breakfast. Pets welcome. Cot available. Laundry and drying facilities. Evening meal from £9.

Restaurant has Welsh and international food. 4 vegan and 7 veggie entrées £2.95-3.65 like deepfried veg with garlic mayo; tomato and orange soup; creamy garlic mushrooms. 7 vegan and 7 veggie main courses £5.89-7.95 like pancake and spinach and broccoli; 'creamy' vegetable crumble; pasta with celery, apricots and walnuts; stuffed mushrooms. At least 4 vegan and 8+ veggie desserts such as steamed treacle or chocolate tart and for vegans blackberry and apple pie, treacle tart, steamed date and walnut. Beer, house wine £6.25, £1.40 glass. Teas or coffee 85p, soya milk and milkshakes.

Directions: from A40 take B4313 at Narberth. Rosebush is 8 miles.

SOUTH GLAMORGAN

Cardiff

Crumbs

33 David Morgan Arcade
Cardiff, South Glamorgan CF1 2AF
Tel: 01222 395 007 Fax:
Open: Mon-Fri 10-15.00, Sat 10-16.00, closed Sun
Vegetarian café. Salads £2.80, spuds from £2.10, soup and bread £2.40, pasta £3.25, curry and chilli £3.40. Desserts include fruit salads, carrot cake and muffins.

The Chapter Arts Centre Cafe

Market Road, Canton, Cardiff
South Glamorgan
Tel: 01222 372 756 Fax:
Open every day 09.00-21.00
Over 50% vegetarian and vegan café café with home-made soup at lunchtime.

Sage Wholefood Restaurant

Wellfield Court, Wellfield Road
Cardiff, South Glamorgan. Tel: 01222 455 437
Open: Mon-Sat 9-18.00, closed Sun

Omnivorous daytime café with some veggie meals from around the world such as pasta, stir fry £4.95, curry, soups £1.95. Some of the dishes are sometimes vegan, for example the pasta can be made with vegan cheese. Occasionally open in the evening by special arrangement for a theme night such as Persian, Italian or French.

Penarth

Tomlins

46 Plassey Street, Penarth
Cardiff, South Glamorgan CF4 8ED. Tel: 01222-706644
Open: Wed-Fri 19.00-00.30. Sat 11-15.00, 19.00-00.30
may open on Tue in future

Vegetarian restaurant with 50% vegan menu that changes weekly. 4 entrées £3.25-3.75 could be tomato summer pudding with garlic, shallots, basil and a raspberry dressing; chestnut and red lentil soup. 4 mains £7.30-7.95 include aubergine moussaka with red bean and onion filling; Mexican pie with salsa and guacamole; mushroom and red wine pate en croute with pine nut sauce; potato rosti with black bean and okra with a red chilli sauce. 2 veggie and 2 vegan desserts £3.30. Beer, house wine £6.90, £1.85 glass. Tea £1.25, coffee £1.45, soya milk. Service not included. Wheelchair access to restaurant but not toilets. Last reservation 22.30.

WEST GLAMORGAN

Swansea

Silver Screen

68a Bryn-y-moor Road, Swansea
West Glamorgan SA1 4JJ, Tel: 01792-412752
Open Tues-Sat 09-17.00, Sun 10-16.30, closed Mon

New vegetarian restaurant and café with a mixture of fast food,

French, Indian, Mediterranean, Mexican, organic and whole-food. Cooked veggie and vegan breakfast till 11.00 £2.75 with veggie bacon, veggie sausage, beans, hash brown, mushrooms, toast, tea and coffee. Homemade soups, pasta dish of the day, starters like homemade paté and toast or hummus £1.95, salads £1.45 (side) £2.95 (full on), toasted sandwiches, jacket potatoes, special of the day, curries, burgers, chilli, stir fries. 2 course Sunday dinner £4.95, choose from soup or dessert. You could have fresh tomato and sage soup with granary bread; cashew and mushroom roast with fresh seasonal veg, roast spuds and parsnip, Yorkshire pud and gravy; then either apple and rhubarb crumble and custard or organic rice pub. Desserts 95p-£1.50 and they have vegan cream, custard, soya milk, yogurt, mayo - hey we love these folk. Tea 65p, coffee 70p.Private parties in the evening such as the local vegan or Buddhist group.

GWENT (MONMOUTHSHIRE)

near Newport

The West Usk Lighthouse

St Brides, Wentloog
near Newport
Gwent NP1 9SF
Tel: 01633-810 126.
1 single £45, 3 doubles £75
Veggie friendly B&B in a grade II listed 1820's lighthouse betwixt Newport and Cardiff with wedge-shaped rooms, waterbed, four posters and a flotation tank. The recently refurbished lantern room can be used for romantic champagne breakfasts, complete with soya milk for vegans. If you're feeling stressed out, aromatherapy and reiki are available. Ideal base for checking out the remarkable Severn Bore, not a tedious resident from over the water but a surfee's dream tidal surge which races upriver for many miles. Bring your board dudes for the Spring and Neap tides.

GWYNEDD

Bangor

Herbs Cookshop

307-309 High St, Bangor
Gwynedd LL57 1BG
Tel: 01248 351 249 Fax:
Open: Mon-Sat 08.00-17.00, closed Sun
Vegetarian café and take-away with some vegan food. Free delivery over £25 within 10 miles, otherwise 20p per mile. Menu 1 for £3.50 is a selection of decorated sandwiches with crisps and salad garnish plus fingers of pizza then chocolate tiffin with fresh fruit. Menu 2 £4 quiche and pizza with choice of three salads, homemade rolls and scones. Menu 3 £4.50 offers a choice of lasange, moussaka, curry or chilli with rice and accompaniements and green salad with rolls, followed by fresh fruit crumble or bread and butter pudding or lemon cheesecake. 10% discount for Vegetarian Society. Outside catering.

Daffryn Ardudwy

Clwt Cotal Helygn

Daffryn Ardudwy, Gwynedd LL44 2 EP
Tel: 01341 247580. Open Easter-October
2 doubles, 1 twin £14.50 per person per day B&B; £75 for 3 nights with 3 course evening meal, £175 weekly with EM. Cottage with twin beds and lounge £18.50 daily, £85 3 nights with EM, £199 weekly with EM. Children sharing under 12 £7.50-9.00, under 2 £3.75-4.50.
Vegetarian and vegan guest house and pottery within the Snowdonia National Park, 5 miles south of the historic town of Harlech. Sit peacefully or walk in their large garden, with ponds and organic vegetable plot, or stroll further to see their coppice wither they are gowing a willow 'house' (room rates available when it's grown). Visit the prehistoric burial cham-

bers only a short walk from the house up through the woods to the sea and beautiful beaches. Walk further up the Roman Steps to the Rhinog Hills, or for a real challenge up Cader Idris (seat of the giant Idris) to see the lake set in the hollow near the top. You may even climb Snowdon itself (by train if you want!) which is 35 miles to the north. Or just come and relax, and enjoy delicious wholesome vegetarian food, cooked by John who was the chef for the Centre for Alternative Technology (35 miles south) and served in pottery made by Linda. Gluten free or any dietary variations and adaptations available.

Capel Curig

Bryn Tyrch Hotel
Capel Curig, Gwynedd LL24 0EL
Tel: 01690-7202223 Fax: 01690-720338
Lively country pub and omnivorous hotel, well known to climbers and walkers since the turn of the century, offering vegetarian and vegan dinner, bed and breakfast as well as a packed lunch if required. 5 miles from Snowdon in the magnificent scenery of the Snowdonia National Park, Capel Curig is the ideal centre for all outdoor pursuits, yet less than 30 miles from the main beaches and attractions of North Wales. 17 double rooms, 8 of them en suite, all with TV. Popular with study and team building groups, clubs and schools.

Conwy

The Wall Place Vegetarian Café
Bishops Yard, Chapel Street
Conwy, Gwynedd LL32
Tel: 01492 596 326 Fax:
Open: Mon-Fri 12-15.00. Sat 12-16.00, 19-22.00. Sun 13-16.00
Main dishes £5.95-6.95, starters £1.95-2.95. Most of the menu is vegan including all the cakes. Sometimes there's a band on Saturday nights, when £10 gets you in and a buffet meal.

Maentwrog

The Old Rectory Hotel
Maentwrog, Gwynedd LL41 4HN
Tel: 01766 590305 Fax: 01766 530305
Restaurant open to non residents every day

Hotel with vegetarian restaurant in a 400 year old Rectory standing in three acres of riverside gardens in the Vale of Ffestiniog. One single en suite and one double en suite £38-59; family room £56. Rooms are large with 5' or 6' beds, tea/coffee making and TV. Also TV lounge and bar. Full English veggie or vegan cooked breakfast. Close to nature walking, Harlech, Portmeirion.

Restaurant offers 3 courses for £12.95. Soups: lentil and coriander, thick veg, tomato, haricot bean and tarragon. Hummus, sweetcorn on the cob, pate, mushrooms in stout batter. Main courses are Arabic special of basmati rice, brown lentils, topped with crispy fried onions, plus chickpeas in tomat, lemon and cummin sauce with potatoes, cauliflower, coriander and oregano; African special of sweet potatoes, sweetcorn and peas with coconut, cummin, onion, garlic and ginger accompanied by savoury rice and cashews; Eastern special with stir-fried veg with cashews, ginger, savoury rice and noodles; savoury pancakes; nut roast; paella; walnut pasta; salad extravaganza. Finish off with fresh fruit salad, homemade apple pie, coffee and welsh liqueur. Italian house wine £8.95, £1.80 glass.

Directions: situated on Dwyryd river bank, A496 to Harlech.

Penisarwaun

Graianfryn   *
Penisarwaun, Gwynedd LL55 3WH
Tel: 01286 871007. a.crawshaw@bangorr.ac.uk
Open all year.

Vegetarian guest house with vegetarian staff. 1 double room £18; 1 double en suite with settee and TV; 1 twin en suite £20.

Tea/coffee facilities in rooms. Veggie and vegan breakfasts with veggie sausages, muesli, soya milk & vegan marg. Evening meal £13.
Homepage: www.ndirect.co.uk/~graianfryn.

Talsarnau

Tremeifion Vegetarian Hotel

Soar Road, Talsarnau
Gwynedd LL47 6UH
Tel: 01766 770491 Fax: 01766 771272
tremeifion@mcmail.com
Open almost all year   £47-54

Vegetarian hotel and restaurant open to non-residents. 1 double room £33, 4 doubles en suite ~~£40/45~~ including full breakfast AND three course dinner with coffee and mints. Tea/coffee making in rooms, hair dryer. Meals all have vegan options using local organic wholefoods where possible. Wide range of organic wines and juices. Packed lunches can be prepared when required. 5 miles of wide, safe, sandy beaches in glori-

ous countryside within easy reach of Snowdon and spectacular views over the estuary towards Portmeirion. Steam railways, castles and wonderful walking.

Restaurant has 10 places. Plenty of vegan food clearly marked. Choice of three starters like organic vegetable juice, fresh tomato soup, baby corn in dill and vegan garlic 'butter', pumpkin soup, creamy vegan butterbean dip with sesame toast. Two mains such as mushroom and leek Bourguignon with rice; cashew and carrot tarte with veg; veg and cashew korma with rice; apricot nut roast with veg; roast tofu and veg with couscous; three layer terrine with veg; all served with vegan salad. Three desserts such as vegan treacle tart, toffee'd bananas, Belgian fruit cake, vegan apple pie. Tea or coffee served in the lounge or conservatory. Beer, house wine £7.75, £1.65 glass. Pot of tea 60p, coffee 75p, soya milk.

POWYS (MONTGOMERY)

Berriew

Bank Farmhouse

Felindre, Berriew
Welshpool, Powys SY21 8QX
Tel: Tel: no phone Fax:
Open beginning of May until end September

Vegetarian bed and breakfast run by an almost vegan in a former hill farm, situated in the peaceful Montgomeryshire countryside, overlooking the Rhin and Severn valleys and with views of the distant Shopshire hills. One twin room £13. TV and tea/coffee making in guests' sitting room. Soya milk available. No evening meal. Packed lunches £2. No smoking. Not suitable for young children. No pets as livestock nearby and resident feline.

Directions: 3 miles from Berriew village, just off the A483 Welshpool-Newtown road. Rough track up to the farmhouse is a bit steep in places and unsuitable for cars. Leave your motor in the small layby at the bottom of the track by the gate, unless you have 4-wheel drive. Landrover can collect visitors with luggage on arrival.

3 miles from the attractive village of Berriew, several times a winner of the Best Kept Village Award. There's a corner shop, post officer, phone, grocer, Andrew Logan Museum of Sculpture and Silver Scenes Jewellery gallery, two pubs, hotel with evening meals, picnic area and walks along the tow-path. Nearby walks include the Kerry Ridgeway, Clyndwr's Way near Welshppol, and the long distance Offa's Dyke footpath. Also near Machynlleth, the Centre for Alternative Technology and Lake Vyrnwy RSPB reserve.

Builth Wells

Trericket Mill
Vegetarian Guesthouse
Erwood, Builth Wells, Powys LD2 3TQ
Tel: 01982 560312 Fax:
1 single £14.50, 2 double £39, 2 twin £29-£39 all en suite, 1 family £25-£42.
Also from £8 for bunk rooms in traditional stone building in the orchard. Some camping pitches (£3.50 per person) as well. Grade II listed former water mill sympathetically restored and retaining a unique historic atmosphere offers a varied vegetarian breakfast menu. Veg or vegan evening meal £10.50. Discount for Vegetarian and Vegan Society. Situated in the Upper Wye Valley, walking and cycling route, pony trekking, canoeing, climbing, gliding etc. Between Brecon, Builth Wells and Hay-On-Wye, set back from A470 1 mile south of Erwood village.

Hyssington

The Old Barn
Hyssington, Nr Churchstoke
Powys SY15 6AT
Tel: 01588 620660 Fax:
Vegetarian guest house. Delightful stone built converted farm building situated in the quiet conservation village of

Hyssington on the Shropshire/Montgomeryshire border offering delicious vegetarian/vegan cuisine. Double £16 per person, another double en suite £18 each. Sitting room. Evening meal on request £9.

Machynlleth

Quarry Shop & Café

13 Heol Maengwyn, Machynlleth
Powys SY20 8EB
Tel: 01654 702 626 Fax: 01654 702 624
Open: Mon-Wed, Fri-Sat 9-16.30, Thu 9-14.00. Sun 10-16.00
summer only.
Vegetarian café and take-away. Soup, hummus, various curreis, pizza, nut roasts, pasta bakes, salads £1.15-4.25. Also trifle, vegan sorbet, cakes including vegan. Teas and coffee 50-70p, soya milk. Prepack soya milkshakes. Bring your own booze, no corkage charge. High chairs, some children's portions, one step wheelchair access. 10% discount in shop only to VSUK and Vegan Society.

Vegetarian Restaurant

Centre for Alternative Technology
Pantperthog, Near Machynlleth, Powys
Tel: 01654 702 400 Fax:
Centre open every day 10-16.00
Vegetarian restaurant open every day 10-15.30, later in summer. Admission to the centre is £3.95 adults, concessions £3, children 5-18 £2.30. Family ticket £10.95 for 2 adults and up to 4 children.

By Alex Bourke and Alan Todd, with an introduction by Roselyne Masselin of *La Cuisine Imaginaire* and foreword by Paul and Linda McCartney.

France is a veggie-lover's paradise, but only if you know where to find it! This **brand new** guide features:

150 places to eat out and crash out, over **20** veggie restaurants in Paris alone, vegetarian hotels and guest houses all over France, all-you-can-eat vegan buffets in Paris and Marseille, veggie vocabulary, maps and cartoons, the hitchhiker's guide to the south of France on 50 francs a day, connect with fellow veggies in France!

Available from bookshops, price £6.99.

Or order direct from Vegetarian Guides Ltd, 32 Brading Rd, London SW2 2AW. Add £1.50 postage first copy, £1 for more. Credit card orders telephone the Vegetarian Society on 0161-928 0793.

VEGETARIAN BRITAIN

NEW RESTAURANT
& ACCOMMODATION FORM

Are you the proprietor of a vegetarian guest house or restaurant not listed in this guide? Then please please tell us about yourselves to ensure your **FREE** listing in the next edition of *Vegetarian Britain*. Please feel free to enclose your menu or brochures - the more you send, the more we'll write! Thanks.

Name of establishment: ....

Proprietor / Manager: ....

Address: ....

....

.... Postcode ....

Phone: .... Fax: ....

Email: ....

Veggie ... Vegan ... Other ....

Restaurant .... Café ... Tea room ... Pub ... Other ....

Hotel ... B&B ... Guest house ... Hostel ... Other ....

Additional info:

Please return to: Vegetarian Guides Ltd,
32 Brading Rd, London SW2 2AW.

VEGETARIAN BRITAIN
READER RESPONSE FORM

We are relying on **YOU** to help make the next edition of *Vegetarian Britain* even better. The best letters will receive a free copy of your choice of one of our guides. Please feel free to continue on as many sheets as you wish. Thanks.

Are there any improvements you'd like to see in the guide?

Any places you would like to see featured in the next edition?

Any places you would like to see chopped out of the next edition, and why?

Any descriptions you would like to see changed?

Where did you buy your guide? _____

Are you: veggie __ vegan __ other _____

Your name: . . . .

Address: . . . .

. . . .

. . . . Postcode . . . .

Please return to: Vegetarian Guides Ltd, 32 Brading Rd, London SW2 2AW.

VEGETARIAN
BRITAIN

By Alex Bourke and Alan Todd
with a foreword by Paul and Linda McCartney

Hankering for a day trip or weekend away and wondering if you should pack a hamper first? Now you can dump the veggie emergency kit, safe in the knowledge that wherever you go, you'll be able to refuel at totally vegetarian and vegan eateries and sleeperies.

This brand new guide features **hundreds of vegetarian restaurants, cafés, hotels and guest houses all over Britain with opening times, prices and full descriptions including what's on the menu for vegans. The most up-to-date, comprehensive and detailed veggie guide ever.**

Available from bookshops, price £7.99. Or order direct from Vegetarian Guides Ltd, 32 Brading Rd, London SW2 2AW.

Credit card orders telephone the Vegetarian Society on 0161-928 0793.

- -

Name: . . . .

Address: . . . .

. . . .

Postcode . . . .   Telephone: . . . .

Please send me ...... copies of *Vegetarian Britain* @£7.99, ... copies of *Vegetarian France* @£6.99, ... copies of *Vegetarian Oz/NZ* @£4.99, ... copies of *Worldwide Vegetarian Guide* @£9.99. Postage and packing: one book add £1.50, then £1 per book. For postage to EC: add 50% of total book order. Other countries add 100% of total book order.
Total for items listed above £ ..... Postage £ ...... TOTAL £ ......
Make cheques/PO payable to Vegetarian Guides Ltd. Sterling payment only.

MERRY CHRISTMAS
HAPPY BIRTHDAY
DIWALI GREETINGS
HAPPY ANNIVERSARY
say it with a
Vegetarian Guide -
the year long gift in the
best possible taste
BON VOYAGE

v

'SUITABLE FOR VEGETARIANS'

It is.   Is it?

The Vegetarian Society's distinctive trademark is recognised

by consumers as the only independent guarantee that

a product is genuinely suitable for vegetarians.

If it's not approved by The Vegetarian Society

it simply isn't up to the mark.

Registered Charity No. 259358

COMING SOON...
new super improved
VEGETARIAN
LONDON 3rd ed

By Alex Bourke and Paul Gaynor

as recommended by Time Out, The Big Issue, Vegan Society, Vegetarian Society, Animal Aid, completely rewritten and updated for 1998-9.

"The Vegetarian Bible for London" containing everything for the Londoner or long-stay visitor. Every vegetarian restaurant and café from Covent Garden to Crouch End, plus a full survey of the many ethnic areas crammed with superb veggie-friendly restaurants and shops.

"A thorough run-down of health and food shops, restaurants serving vegetarian food, green shops and places to buy cruelty-free cosmetics and clothes." **Time Out**

"For people living in or visitng the capital, this book is more important than the A-Z." **The Vegetarian Society**

"From Wood Green to Wimbledon, the book is a comprehensive catalogue of the best restaurants, shops and tourist attractions in the capital." **The Big Issue**

"By the time I've tried every food in every place in this book I'll be 196 years old. You'll have no trouble finding nosh with this remarkably thorough guide to everything vegetarian in London. So join me, get out there and get scoffing!" **Tony Banks, MP**

Available Summer 1998, £5.99

FOOD NUTRIENT CHART

IRON

0-3 months	1.7 mg/day
7-12 months	7.8 mg/day
7-10 years	8.7 mg/day
Average male adult	8.7 mg/day
Average female adult	14.8 mg/day

Tofu

Beans & Pulses

esp: pinto lentils Baked Beans (haricots)

Spinach

Cabbage

Wheatgerm

Wholegrains

Parsley

Prunes & Dates

Dried Apricots

Pumpkin Seeds

Millet

Blackstrap Molasses

(1 tbs = 3.2 mg)

CALCIUM

0-1 year	525 mg/day
7-10 years	550 mg/day
11-18 years	900 mg/day
Average adult	700 mg/day

Tofu (4oz = 150mg calcium)

Tahini (rich source)

Green Leafy Vegetables

Parsley

Watercress

Broccoli

Swede

Almonds

Brazils

Figs

Soya Milk

(fortified eg: Provamel 140 mg/100 gm)

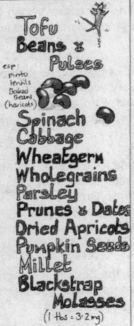

FOOD NUTRIENT CHART

PROTEIN

1-3 years 14-53/day
4-6 years 19-73/day
7-10 years 28-33/day
Average adult 45-50 g/day (approx 2 oz)

Tofu & Rice
(soya/bean/lentils)

Beans / Pulses & Wholegrains
(eg: Beans on toast)

Soya Milk Cereals

Tahini & Pulse
(eg: Hummous)

Beansprouts & Wholegrains

NB Protein needs are automatically met by balanced, varied diet.
There is even protein in potatoes...

B₁₂ *

BEST STEAMED OR EAT RAW —
1-3 years 0.5 mcg/day
Average adult 1.5 mcg/day
IMPORTANT! ESPECIALLY FOR CHILDREN
(there is some evidence that B₁₂
are made by intestinal flora)

Many fortified products:
eg: Soya milks
(Plamil & Unisoy)

Sosmix breakfast cereals
(animal-free)

Margarine
(animal-free)

Soya Mince

Seaweed (eg: Kelp)

Miso

Yeast Extract
(fortified: eg: MERIDIAN)

FOOD NUTRIENT CHART page 3

The previous pages are extracts of a brilliant full colour, illustrated, wipe clean Vegan Food Nutrient wall chart produced by Liz Cooke. Liz has a Catering degree specialising in nutrition, plus 20 years research experience. She tours the country speaking in schools on behalf of all the leading vegan, vegetarian and animal rights organisations.

The complete chart (88 x 18cm) gives recommended daily requirements and vegan sources of:

protein, essential fatty acids, vitamins (A, B, B12, C, D, E, K), minerals (iron, calcium, zinc, iodine, magnesium, phosphorous, sulphur, potassium), carbohydrate and fibre.

Colourful and well illustrated, the chart will fascinate your fiends and educate you and the kids. Order yours at the bargain basement price of £1 each plus p&p: 50p on one copy, £1.50 on 10, £2.50 on 20, £3.50 on 30, £6.50 on 100. Cheques payable to: Steward Distribution, 44 Park Crescent Terrace, Brighton BN2 3HE.